WHOLE CHILD

PARENTING

AGE FOUR

Concept by Claudia Sandor

WHOLE CHILD

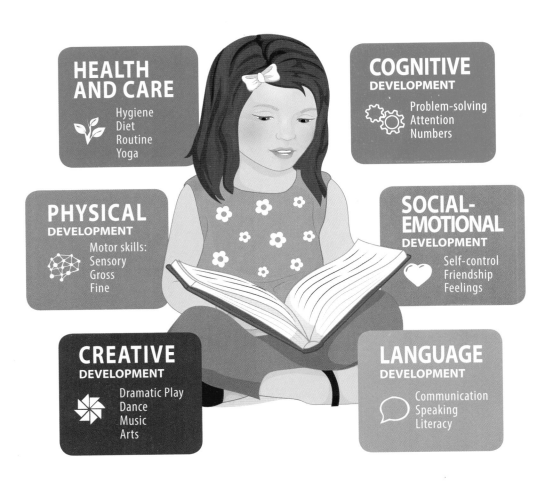

HEALTH AND CARE

Hygiene
Diet
Routine
Yoga

COGNITIVE
DEVELOPMENT

Problem-solving
Attention
Numbers

PHYSICAL
DEVELOPMENT

Motor skills:
Sensory
Gross
Fine

SOCIAL-EMOTIONAL
DEVELOPMENT

Self-control
Friendship
Feelings

CREATIVE
DEVELOPMENT

Dramatic Play
Dance
Music
Arts

LANGUAGE
DEVELOPMENT

Communication
Speaking
Literacy

WHOLE CHILD:
AGE FOUR
Six Areas of Development

WHOLE CHILD

whole \hōl\ **child** \chi-əld\ *compound noun*
1 : a child who is completely developed in all six areas

A **whole child**
grows up to reach
his or her full potential.

A whole child is a **well-rounded** person and lifelong learner.

A whole child is ready to face the world with **confidence.**

A whole child has **self-esteem, knowledge,** and **creativity**.

A whole child will live a **happy** and **fulfilling life**.

Being a successful parent starts with understanding your child.

The Whole Child Parenting Program covers every aspect of a child's cognitive, social-emotional, language, creative, physical, and health and care development.

By using clear examples, color-coded stages, simple and logical steps, age-appropriate materials and toys, developmentally appropriate activities and workbooks, and core parenting books, the Whole Child Program will change the way you think about learning.

Welcome to parenting for the new millenium!

Published by Whole Child Parenting, Inc.
Whole Child Parenting books, activity books, toys, and materials are
available at special discounts when purchased in bulk for premiums
and sales promotions as well as for fundraising or educational use.
For details, please contact us at:
sales@wholechild.co

Whole Child is a registered trademark of Whole Child, LLC
Library of Congress Control Number: 2016905517
ISBN 978-1-944930-05-9

Created by the Whole Child Education Team with:
Early Childhood Education Specialist, Erin Weekes
Book design by Willabel Tong
Art direction by Dan Marmorstein
Editorial direction by Editorial Services of Los Angeles

Visit us on the web at: www.wholechild.co
Email us at: publishing@wholechild.co

Printed in the United States of America.
1 3 5 7 9 10 8 6 4 2

Contents

What Is Whole Child Parenting?

It Is Parenting from Head to Toe

Whole child parenting involves exposing your child to everything he needs to be happy, healthy, well adjusted, smart, and developing right on track. A whole child is a well-rounded person, someone whose innate talents have been developed in every major milestone category and who is ready to face the world with confidence. A whole child has the self-esteem and knowledge to develop his true potential.

Whole child parenting is you doing what you can, with our help, to get him there. The Whole Child Parenting Program is for busy people just like you. With interactive materials that support you at every step, using toys, workbooks, activities, videos, web support, and an app, the Whole Child Parenting Program takes into account the whole child and helps you, the parent or primary caregiver, do what is necessary and best for your child at every stage, every age from infancy to five years old. It helps you parent with a purpose, giving you practical advice and materials that explain the whys and how-tos and goals of each step you take to help your child grow.

Whole child parenting is a process that begins with you. It can be overwhelming to think about the responsibility you have to your child in one of the most important years of your child's life.

This fourth year is a crucial year because development, in both the body and brain, is happening at a rapid pace. This fourth year will continue to set the stage for how your child problem solves, communicates, socializes, and thinks for the rest of his life. That is not to say that you won't have amazing experiences with your child when he is four. You will have absolutely transformative experiences with your four-year-old child during these next twelve months. You will get to see life from the perspective of a person who is just over three feet tall! And **your presence and influence will always matter the most in this fourth year.** The world is constantly changing; will your child be ready for the global economy years from now? Just by reading this book you are setting yourself along the right path for being the best parent you can be for your four-year-old child.

HOW TO GET ON THE RIGHT TRACK NOW?

Whole Child Parenting: Age Four has six chapters for the six areas of development seen in the column at right. **Each area of development is assigned its own color.**

Each of the six chapters begins with a chart and summary to introduce you to the concepts and terminology in the pages ahead. Within each chapter, **you will also get real-life activities and insights that paint a picture of how your child demonstrates these developmental concepts**

1 Cognitive
Development

2 Social Emotional
Development

3 Language
Development

4 Creative
Development

5 Physical
Development

6 Health and Care

in everyday life. In addition to examples, there are tips and advice for parents and primary caregivers to use to support and guide you as you and your child encounter and master each of the upcoming milestones.

The Whole Child Parenting Program has developed five smart, modern, easy steps to help you raise a happy, thriving child.

> ## The Whole Child Parenting Program involves:
>
> 1. **Committing yourself**
> 2. **Educating yourself**
> 3. **Creating the right environment**
> 4. **Using the right materials**
> 5. **Staying on track**

That's it. Five steps to making your experience with your child the most rewarding and productive experience in your life.

STEP ONE: COMMITTING YOURSELF

Let's start with commitment. As a parent you have already taken the huge step of accepting responsibility for the little person in front of you. What is next required might not even be a step that needs articulating for you, but it bears repeating here: **You need to commit quality time to raising your whole child.**

There is no formula or script when it comes to being successful in parenting. Many parents look to doctors, textbooks, and experts for the secrets to parenting success. And while all of these are great sources, none address the whole child. And the whole child needs your attention.

Each child is different and has a different temperament, dif- ferent interests, and a different personality. As a parent, you are also different. Every parent has different values that come from being a part of different cultures, socioeconomic classes, education levels, religions, and family sizes. The best way to be successful in parenting is to be involved with your child. By being involved and communicating with your child, you are better able to support her and her needs.

Many wonder what the real measures and outcomes of good parenting are. It does not involve your child having a high IQ, being talented in sports, or making a lot of money. Good parenting results in raising a child who grows up to give back to society, is independent, has a good work ethic, gets along well with others, and understands her identity and self-worth.

When it comes to measuring your success as a parent, it is important to look at the quality of the relationship you have with your child and not how effectively you can control your child. Just because your child listens and follows the rules does not mean she understands or respects them; it just means she is obedient.

The quality of your relationship has to do with your involvement and communication with your child. Know what guidelines are appropriate to set for your child, and explain them in a way that shows why these rules are necessary and important. As a parent, you need to meet your child's needs and help her feel respected. This can be done by explaining the reasons behind rules and discussing your child's feelings and opinions.

When your child feels like she is a valued member of the family and the community, she will then develop the confidence needed to begin moving toward being independent and making her own decisions.

Parents who are uninvolved with their children tend to make their children feel ignored and unvalued. At the same time, parents who are overly controlling and establish strict rules over all avenues of their children's lives tend to make their children feel stressed and have low self-esteem. It is important to find the middle ground between controlling your child and overlooking your child.

Your child is born naturally impulsive, immature, and ambitious, and she looks to you for guidance and support. This is why it is important to **make sure you communicate clear guidelines and expectations** for your child to alleviate stress and misunderstandings.

THE FOUR STYLES OF PARENTING

Whole Child Parenting: Age Four combines research, expert advice, and firsthand experience. In the past few decades, early childhood education has grown exponentially.

In the late 1950s, psychologist Erik Erikson organized development from birth to death into eight stages; according to Erikson, a person cannot successfully excel in the next stage of life without first completing the stage before.

Looking specifically at the first three stages, which cover ages birth to five, we see that a person's success lies first in his relationship with his parents. **Stage 1,** covering ages birth to two years old, focuses on a child's ability to develop **trust** with his parents. From there, children move on to **Stage 2** (for ages two to four years old), when the child is developing autonomy. **Autonomy** is your child's sense of self as an individual. Your child develops a sense of self by exploring the environment, learning about his own interests, and testing his limits. Moving forward to **Stage 3** (ages four to five years old), your child is **finding his purpose and place** within the family.

In the last 40 years, developmental psychologists have established **four styles of parenting.** The best parenting style is a combination of these four parenting styles—one in which you approach different situations with different solutions and always communicate with your child.

Authoritarian Parenting

The authoritarian parenting style can best be described as strict. Authoritarian parents tend to set rules that result in rewards or punishment if they are not followed. Rules are not explained and usually follow a reasoning of "because I said so." **These parents usually set high demands and expect obedience** but are not very responsive to their children. Children who grow up under the authoritarian parenting style tend to be obedient and usually well performing in school but socially exhibit signs of shame, low self-esteem, and lowered happiness levels.

Authoritative Parenting

The authoritative parenting style establishes rules and guidelines for children instead of just demands. Authoritative parents are more nurturing and forgiving, rather than simply punishing. They are responsive to their children and willing to listen and answer questions.

An important quality of authoritative parents is that they create clear standards for their children and adjust those standards based on their children's conduct.

Children who grow up under the authoritative parenting style tend to be capable and successful at learning new things. Socially and emotionally, they feel accepted and tend to be happy.

Permissive Parenting

The permissive parenting style is one that has few demands or guidelines. Parents tend to have low expectations for their children's maturity and abilities. **Permissive parents are more lenient with rules, preferring to avoid confrontation.**

This parenting style is usually nurturing and communicative but leaves children looking at their parent as more of a friend. Children who grow up under the permissive parenting style tend to often have poor self-regulation skills and may experience problems with authority and have trouble in school.

Uninvolved Parenting

The uninvolved parenting style is one with even fewer demands as well as little communication and responsiveness. Uninvolved parents fulfill their children's basic needs but tend to be detached and unavailable for their children in all other areas.

Children who grow up under the uninvolved parenting style tend to have low self-esteem, a hard time regulating their emotions, and a hard time making friends.

Your child's personality and temperament play a major role in how you choose your parenting style. Research shows correlations between parenting styles and their impact on children. There is also evidence showing other factors, such as a child's personality and the outside environment, playing a role as well. Your larger environment—such as culture, religion, socio-economic class, and family style—can also affect how your child reacts to your parenting. School, friends, and personality play a significant role in how your child responds to your parenting style.

It is important to be consistent with your parenting style, especially when it comes to discipline and setting expectations for your child. Besides taking into account her environment, think about other people in your child's life, such as your spouse or partner or caregiver. Take time to talk to each other about parenting styles and how you will work together when raising your child. Talk about what you both value as important and how you were each raised; this is important for keeping your parenting style consistent.

At the end of the day, you need to remember to be present and realistic. **Be present both physically and mentally in order to be responsive to your child's needs.** Be realistic in your expectations and the guidelines you set for your child.

Committing quality time as a parent, whichever parenting style(s) you choose, is the single most important factor in your child's healthy development.

STEP TWO: EDUCATING YOURSELF

Addressing the whole child means knowing about the general developmental milestones your child will experience at each age. Milestones define peak stages of accomplishment when your child achieves the end of one stage before moving on to the next. **Milestones are exciting, because when a child reaches one you get to see how far she has come.** And you get to look forward to the next amazing stage your whole child will go through.

But how can you be aware of milestones without knowing the specific developmental categories the stages occur in? How can you have realistic expectations about what is age appropriate and what your whole child should or should not be doing? *Whole Child Parenting: Age Four* lays out six major developmental areas of your child's growth and follows them through this year of your child's development.

Cognitive development

The first area of development is cognitive development. Cognitive development refers to the process of learning and the growth of intelligence and other mental capabilities, such as memory, reasoning, problem solving, and thinking. Memory and problem solving play a large role in your child's ability to engage in science, mathematical thinking, and logic.

Your involvement strengthens your child's cognitive abilities over these next years and plays a significant role in her school readiness and how she will learn and retain information later in life. At birth, your child's brain is only a quarter of the size of an adult brain; by age five, it has grown to be close to the same size and volume as yours.

Take advantage of these first five years to set the path and exercise the brain to its fullest potential. The Whole Child Parenting Program will very clearly define the stages of cognitive development and will help you be involved in your child's growth in this area.

Social-emotional development

Social-emotional skills reflect how effectively your child is able to interact in social settings. In order to interact well he must develop positive relationships. He must learn to recognize and regulate his emotions and reactions while communicating his feelings.

For young children, social-emotional skills provide a pivotal foundation upon which are built a range of other skills that are necessary in preschool as well as on play dates. Development in this category will help to determine how well your child succeeds with peer interaction throughout his life.

In order to interact well with others your child must develop positive relationships with others. He must also effectively coordinate his actions with communicating his feelings. As well, he must learn to recognize and regulate his emotions and reactions in many different social settings.

Your child needs to have good self-regulatory skills (i.e. the ability to calm himself down), keen emotional understanding (i.e. learning with help what made him feel the way he does), and growing communication skills such as naming how he feels and dealing with those feelings.

Language development

Language development is how your child communicates, from basic sounds and gestures to the use of pictures in books and words for speaking. As she ages your child will be communicating more than her emotions and needs. She will begin to tell stories, ask questions, and describe people and objects.

Your child will use memory to remember words and past events when telling stories. At an early age, your child's memory will also play a role in symbolic play when she uses props and objects as symbols to represent her ideas. These symbols will later translate to letter recognition and emerging literacy.

The Whole Child Parenting Program identifies how to use sign language to support early literacy skills, and we also include signs in supplemental and supportive materials in the program. Sign language for communication plays a role in your child's social-emotional development because it makes her better able to convey her emotions and needs when she is largely preverbal.

Creative development

Creative development involves how your child uses music, art, movement, and dramatic play to express himself and build imaginative thinking. When doing art, let your child make a mess and indulge in all the different textures and materials you provide. Make a paintbrush or other tools available to your child and then let him explore the paint with his hands.

Creative development plays a big role in your child's physical development as well. Music and movement build your child's gross motor skills (big muscles) by allowing your child to test balance and large body movements. Visual art builds your child's fine motor skills (small muscles) by allowing him to explore materials such as scissors, paintbrushes, and crayons.

Creative development can be used as an avenue for social-emotional development. Through art and dramatic play, your child can express and act out feelings, model behavior, or work through emotions.

Through activities, examples, and tips, *Whole Child Parenting: Age Four* shows how important creative development can be to your child's other areas of development as well.

Physical development

Physical development refers to your child's control over fine motor skills (small muscle movements of fingers, toes, and wrists) and gross motor skills (bigger movements that use the large muscles in the arms, legs, and torso). Between birth and five years old, your child's body and motor abilities make great strides.

Physical development has a lot to do with your child's self-esteem and sense of trust. Your child is more willing to test her physical skills of throwing, kicking, and balancing when she feels comfortable and confident within her environment.

Physical development is important because it plays a large role in children developing independence and self-help skills. Getting dressed, feeding themselves, and cleaning up are all skills that involve both fine and gross motor skills, which, when combined, develop sensory motor skills.

The Whole Child Parenting Program explains how your child's physical changes correlate with the development of motor abilities and overall physical growth and development.

Health and care

This section discusses safety, grooming, self-help, and the health of your child. As your child grows older, he will be more independent with his hygiene, from small achievements like brushing his own teeth to bigger accomplishments like potty training.

As he goes through each developmental stage, your child's body is changing and growing at a swift pace. He is growing taller, sprouting new teeth, and becoming more active, which will reflect in changes in his diet each year.

Whole child parenting also involves using yoga. Yoga is a great resource in which to engage your child from infancy through age four and beyond. Not only does it allow your child to explore his balance, but it also strengthens his social-emotional development by helping him find an avenue to calm himself. Yoga can also provide a bonding experience for parent and child.

Reaching Milestones

An important and exciting addition to our exploration of the six developmental categories is the Reaching Milestones section we provide at the end of the book. This assessment list will allow you to see everything your child should be doing and accomplishing developmentally around that age. Milestone assessments provide an exciting reflection of all that you are doing to support your whole child.

STEP THREE: CREATING THE RIGHT ENVIRONMENT

Now that you have committed your time and started educating yourself, it is time to follow through by setting up the right environment. Setting up an environment where your whole child will thrive plays a large role in all six areas of their development.

The importance of play
We are in a day and age in which there is an abundance of technology and information available to us. It is hard to remember a time when an answer to a question wasn't a mouse click away or we couldn't watch a video about how to fix something.

Technology has made our lives so much easier over the years, but that is not the case when it comes to our little ones. **Young children need to have the opportunity to make their own connections and discoveries within their environment.** Children between the ages of birth and three learn the most through play.

When setting up an environment that fosters **free play**, it is important to have child-sized furniture as well as incorporate baskets and trays for storing toys. Child-sized furniture and organizational materials such as bins and trays for different categories of toys help your child build independence and self-help skills. Being able to pick what he wants to play with from the shelf or bin will build upon your child's personal interests.

Just because your child is more in control of what activity and materials he is exploring in free play does not mean that you do not need to be involved in free play with your child. Setting up learning and play environments and making learning materials available is just part of encouraging free play. When watching your child explore materials in free play, it is important to interact with him.

The main aspect to remember about free play is that your child's interests guide it.

Structured play is also an important type of play and can help foster and build specific skills. Structured play differs from free play based on the fact that you are planning the activity and materials in which your child is engaging. You are leading the way with a specific activity that has a specific goal. Examples of structured activities can be doing a science experiment with your child or sorting different colored blocks. It is important to have both a combination of structured and free play activities available for your child.

Indoor environments

Incorporating child-sized furniture as well as baskets and trays for storing toys helps your child build independence and self-help skills.

Trays and baskets allow you to provide more manipulatives (age appropriate toys that foster growth) for your child and make it easier for your child to help care for and clean her environment. **When furniture and materials are at your child's eye level, she is able to have better control of her physical movements and be more aware of her environment.**

When setting up an environment that is beneficial for your child's language skills, it is important to have age-appropriate books available. Your child's interest in books both while reading with you as well as pretending to read on her own helps her relate words to pictures. Take your child's language learning to the next level and place labels like TABLE on your kitchen table. Your child will start making the connection between words and objects.

When doing art, let your child get messy and indulge in all the different textures and materials you provide. Investing in an easel, putting down a tarp, providing a smock, or buying washable paint can help you make your indoor environment fit for creative exploration. Having some paper and crayons out on a table that is child-sized makes expressing herself and her ideas easy. She can use the crayons to express herself creatively and create symbols that depict her feelings or needs.

Besides art materials, your child can express her thoughts and feelings through dramatic play by modeling roles and situations when dressing up or using props. Having a mirror in your child's room allows her to explore her self-concept skills. You will find your child making different faces in the mirror or watching herself stack blocks. Having a mirror that is at your child's eye level builds her self-concept by developing a better understanding of herself as an individual who has her own interests and ideas. Don't overwhelm your child with too many choices or structured activities, but instead follow your child's needs and interests to help encourage independence.

Your commitment to your child is very important when it comes to building attention span and memory skills. Having a rug or a chair that is child-sized will make your child more comfortable and thus want to spend longer on an activity. Your child's attention span is a cognitive skill, and it grows as your child grows older.

The Whole Child Parenting Program provides you with all the guidelines, furniture, educational books, activities, supplies, and toys for your whole child's stimulating environment.

Outdoor environments

Environments where your child can engage in free play allow him to develop self-identity and develop his own interests. He is able to learn more about himself by testing his cognitive and physical limits. There aren't always many opportunities for your child to fully engage in free play at home, which is why **outdoor environments provide beneficial play spaces for your child.**

By its nature, play is flexible, changeable, and multifaceted, so your child's play environment should reflect those criteria as well. Play is a core and vital component of how young children learn. Structured and unstructured play provide health benefits by allowing your child to be physically active as well as engaging in problem-solving and creative exploration.

Outdoor environments provide space and opportunities for structured activities that help children learn to communicate and work together, while unstructured activities in large, open areas help your child push the limits and take risks.

Your child can make a mess, climb, shout, jump, and run as fast as he wants in open spaces. He can fully express himself and explore his body's movements. From this, your child will develop a sense of competence and confidence in his own physical abilities.

Large, open areas provide opportunities for your child to be creative and use his imagination. He can make connections and witness vivid colors, patterns, and textures in an outdoor environment.

Without material items, media, or structured rules, children can create their own games, engage in dramatic play, and entertain themselves through the use of their mighty imagination.

Nature provides an abundance of science and math opportunities that your child can explore and manipulate. Problem solving, learning cause and effect, and investigating use all of your child's senses. Your child will be exposed to nature and its elements and make connections by witnessing weather, ecology, growth, and natural life cycles. He can explore what happens when he throws a rock in a pond, adds water to dirt or sand, or watches snow melt.

It is not always easy to find a safe outdoor environment for your child. For families in the city, it may mean you need to travel a little farther, but the benefits are worth it. Outdoor environments can actually be considered cleaner than indoor environments, especially when it comes to germs.

By being in a large space with richly fresh air, germs and infectious agents are spread out. Indoor spaces tend to be more enclosed, which leaves bacteria to sit on surfaces and linger. Overall, the benefits of outdoor environments are enormous, and you need to take advantage of them.

How you set up your child's indoor and outdoor environments plays a large role in how he learns and develops. It is important to remember that you are a part of his environment and **in order for your child to thrive, he needs both a rich learning environment and your involvement.**

STEP FOUR: USING THE RIGHT MATERIALS

As parents, we frequently buy and invest in products and toys that are not age appropriate and serve no purpose developmentally, which is why the Whole Child Parenting Program has created developmentally appropriate tools and materials for the whole child that are both fun and educational.

When starting the Whole Child Parenting Program from infancy, you are able to build and adjust your child's environment and learning materials as she grows older. Many materials, such as toys and furniture, are able to grow with your child from infancy to kindergarten. Other materials, such as Whole Child Parenting activity books, toys, and parent resources, assist you with staying on track with your child's development while also helping you plan and measure your time and commitment to your child. The Whole Child Parenting Program is here to walk with you through these first five years.

A variety and quantity of materials are needed to accommodate young children's short attention spans. Children learn through concrete activities, and parents must be able to provide activities for both their physical, active needs and calm, quiet needs.

Having the right environment with both active and quiet play can help your child's social-emotional development by encouraging self-regulating skills. Having a quiet area to go to when your child feels overstimulated or needs a break is just as essential as having a safe area for her to be active and test her physical and creative limits.

A variety of materials is required to stimulate the development of each age group. Some materials may fit into one or more categories; for example, an art activity can also serve as a fine motor exercise, and dramatic play can also act as a social-emotional tool.

It is important to remember that in order for your child to be able to explore and manipulate materials, she needs to have the materials made easily available to her at all times of the day. Setting up the right environment and investing in furniture that is both safe and easily accessible will play an important role in supporting your child's development.

STEP FIVE: STAYING ON TRACK

Once you have set up your environment, the Whole Child Parenting Program makes staying on track easier by providing you with activity books, toys, and learning materials. **Consistency and routine play a big role in your whole child's development,** so it is up to you to follow through and use these materials with your child.

Five years may seem far away, but time always has a way of sneaking up on us. In the blink of an eye, your child will be five years old and boarding the bus for school. This is a big milestone in your child's life, but you will be confident your child is ready for school because the Whole Child Parenting Program has helped you stay on track with your child's development. Your child is leaving for school a confident, happy, healthy learner.

In the end, all we want for our children is for them to be happy and confident because happiness and confidence set your child on the road to success. The Whole Child Parenting Program is here to get you to that point so you can take a deep breath and know your child is ready to face the world.

Through our *Whole Child Parenting: Age Four* **book, educational materials, and workbooks, tips, and activities, apps, videos, and web support, you will have the tools to build a relationship with your child** that allows him to confidently express himself through his creative and social-emotional skills, which in turn help him build his cognitive, language, and physical skills. You want your child to be healthy, happy, and complete, developing at or ahead of the curve. The Whole Child Parenting Program was developed for you, the committed and caring parent.

four >

Milestones for a Four Year Old

 **COGNITIVE** 1

- Focuses attention more
- Uses five senses to learn math concepts
- Uses spatial language
- Uses problem-solving skills
- Memory and recall improve

 SOCIAL-EMOTIONAL 2

- Builds strong peer ties
- Uses language to express feelings and thoughts
- Controls emotions better
- Develops positive self-esteem and self-identity

 LANGUAGE 3

- Attention span increases
- Understands and comprehends meanings
- Uses around 1,500 words
- Gains phonetic knowledge and writing skills

 CREATIVE 4

- Creates music and responds to music patterns
- Creates and invents new forms of art
- Dances and performs other body movements

 PHYSICAL 5

- Hand-eye coordination skills develop
- Uses senses to guide locomotion
- Balance and endurance increase

 HEALTH AND CARE 6

- Better understands healthful lifestyles
- Is independent with self-help skills
- Understands some other cultures

four

Welcome to age four! This is a year with great changes in your child's growing independence as well as in your relationship with your child. This year will bring more than just problem solving but also reasoning skills and curiosity. Age four is a great time to start communicating openly and comfortably with your child about all the questions and concerns he can articulate about himself and his environment and those in it.

1. Cognitive Development

> **Cognitive development refers to the building of thinking methods, which includes how your child will remember, problem solve, and make decisions from now and into adulthood.**

At age four your child is now able to focus his attention more accurately and is less influenced by distractions, which is important because it will enable him to complete and engage in more challenging tasks. The eagerness to ask questions increases as your child develops a strong curiosity about the world around him.

By this age, your child will have increased memory, which accounts for a big part of his learning capability. This increase in memory supports your child in retaining more and different information at the same time.

Cognitive development at this age includes your child learning more about cause and effect as well as similarities and differences through everyday activities. Cognitive skills are at the forefront of your child's ability to process information, pay attention, memorize, and perform many other learning tasks.

The following chart provides you with an image that walks you through your child's stages of intellectual development.

Understanding these areas of cognitive development will help you learn how your child thinks, how to support learning, and how to teach new skills.

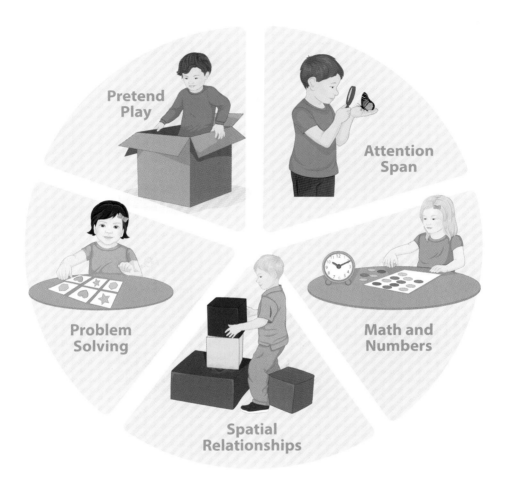

WHOLE CHILD: AGE FOUR
Cognitive
Development Components

Attention Span >
Concentration and Focus

Attention span involves the amount of time your child is able to concentrate and focus on a single activity.

If your child fails to develop strong attention skills, she will have problems with everything from math to social relationships.

Your child now has the ability to focus her attention more accurately and will be less influenced by distractions going on around her, which is important because this will enable her to engage in and complete more challenging tasks later on.

ACTIVITY

Sam and Mom are sitting at the table. Mom pulls out one of Sam's favorite memory games. "Are you ready to play Animal Memory?" says Mom. "Yes, I am!" Sam takes out the 12 game tiles, flips them all over face down, scrambles them up, and arranges them into a grid. Sam goes first, by flipping over two tiles at a time. "Aw, I got a zebra and an elephant," Sam says. "It's your turn, Mom!" Her eyes wander to her electronic tablet. Mom takes her turn and gets a zebra and a goat. "Sam, over here, it's your turn!" says Mom. Sam proceeds to turn over a tile; the first one she gets is a lion. She pauses for a moment, then turns over another tile, getting a giraffe. "Sam, did you notice what my tiles were?" says Mom. Sam says, "Zebra and . . . elephant?"

Left brain activities to do with your child to develop attention skills:

1. This is the first and most important activity to do. Change your child's diet by reducing sugar, increasing raw vegetables and fruit, using fewer processed foods, and increasing the amount of water your child drinks. A simple change of the diet makes a tremendous difference in your child's attention span.

2. Take five to 10 minutes each day to listen to music such as Mozart and Putumayo's *World Sing Along*. Talk about one instrument in the music (for example, piano or drums); this will require your child to pay attention and listen for the instrument. You may ask, "Did you hear the drums play fast or slowly?"

3. Play a game once a week of stacking blocks, then build in another day the following week, and continue till you are doing building projects a bunch of times a week. You would start this game by gathering six blocks, stack them any way you like, and then have your child copy you. This will require focus and attention to stack the blocks like yours.

INSIGHT

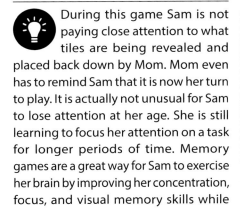

During this game Sam is not paying close attention to what tiles are being revealed and placed back down by Mom. Mom even has to remind Sam that it is now her turn to play. It is actually not unusual for Sam to lose attention at her age. She is still learning to focus her attention on a task for longer periods of time. Memory games are a great way for Sam to exercise her brain by improving her concentration, focus, and visual memory skills while increasing her attention span. As Sam grows older and the two of them play more memory games, she will become better and better at using her new skills in other areas of his development, such as in math.

Attention is a very sophisticated skill; the average attention span for your child is five to 15 minutes. This seems like a short time by adult standards; however, it is a perfect amount of time for your child to focus on one concept or activity without distraction or loss of concentration. Five minutes is long enough to listen to a story, and 15 minutes is long enough to do an art activity, such as cooking something together. Typically the more hands-on an activity is the longer your child will pay attention.

Take a moment and reflect on an activity you have observed your child engaging in, something simple like coloring in a coloring book. Was he able to stay focused and color the entire picture without stopping for a period of time? Or did he constantly stop after each stroke of a color placed on the paper? When your child has to use too much energy to stay focused on his work, then this is a learning block for him.

You may say to yourself, "It is just a coloring page, he can sit without moving around when he watches TV." TV and videos require little energy for your child because he finds these to be interesting but largely undemanding. A coloring page requires effort as your child has to think and focus on staying near the lines, using different colors, and trying to color in one direction. A short attention span will cause task avoidance, meaning that your child will not want to do it no matter how interesting you think it is.

We discussed earlier that your child has about a five to 15 minute attention span; however, one must understand that this does not hold true for all four year olds, because every child develops differently. When this is the case, parents play a key role in helping their children develop their attention skills.

Instead of getting frustrated or labeling your child as having an "attention problem," there are strategies parents should do to increase attention span. *Avoid flooding your child with a lot of options, as this will create distractions and disrupt your child from paying attention.*

Following strategies like those on the next page gives a child brain balance and thus supports the development of his attention span, which will serve him throughout his life in all areas of development and interaction.

Strategies to increase your child's attention skills:

1. Help your child pay longer attention to an activity using toys he likes. If he likes his figurines or stuffed animals, line them up in a row, and ask him to point out certain details in the stuffed animal or figurine (e.g. size, shape, and color).

2. Use daily routines to build attention span. When going to the grocery store talk about the process as you are driving. "We will drive to the store, get a shopping cart, go over to the fresh fruit area, and pick out strawberries. After we have our fruit, we will go to check out, pay, load the car, and then drive back home." Have your child repeat the process back to you to see how well he was paying attention.

3. Help your child slow down. At this age he wants to move around quickly from one activity to another and sometimes without completing what he was working on in the first place. Do a game of Slow Motion. Ask your child to slowly walk to an object on the floor, pick it up, and bring it to you. Ask your child to count the steps as he goes along; this will increase the complexity of the task.

Math and Numbers >
Mathematical Thinking

Math and number awareness involves your child recognizing numbers, counting, learning one-to-one correspondence, recognizing patterns, sorting and classifying.

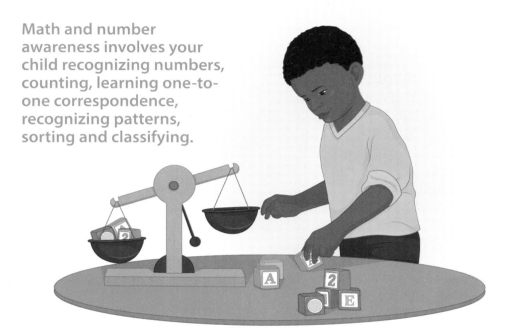

ACTIVITY

Matthew is at the table with his blocks and a new scale that was given to him by his dad. He decides to try it out by putting several blocks in one of the scale baskets. As he continues to add blocks, Matthew begins to see that the basket is tipping to one side and is full. Matthew then decides to pick up more blocks and add those to the other side of the scale.

INSIGHT

In this scenario Matthew is demonstrating his ability to measure and weigh blocks as he figures out how he can get balance on both sides of the scale. Measuring and weighing are math activities; they allow him to think mathematically and strengthen his math skills. Parents can support their child by asking questions during the activity (e.g. "Why do you think the scale is tipping?").

Math and number awareness comprise the foundation for learning more advanced math concepts.

Even before your child starts school, he is developing an understanding of math concepts through everyday interactions (as your child walks up the stairs he counts each step). Mathematical thinking involves your child using his brain to play with the concepts of parts and wholes. Mathematical thinking also occurs when your child becomes fascinated by the insides of things and how different parts make the whole thing work (e.g. puzzles).

Early in your child's life, he was learning about math by using his senses and body to make sense of the environment. When your child held your hand and saw that yours was big while his was small, this demonstrated an early math skill. This experience was preparing him for understanding and naming *small*, *big*, and *bigger*—all mathematical concepts—when he got older. Everything you will see your child do from this point forward will be more complicated.

Engaging in mathematical talk using quantity words *more* and *less* supports math thinking skills.

It is hard to imagine that your child can develop such comprehensive early math skills, but he can. Using mathematical thinking skills includes his working not only on counting numbers, but also learning about geometry, measurement, algebra, data analysis, and probability.

Encourage your child's mathematical thinking and understanding during play. Ask your child questions such as "What can you do to make your tower taller?" or "How many dolls did you put in the crib?"

Math is part of everyday life for your child, meaning you can provide a lot of opportunities for your child to think about math and to physically engage in math through regular routines.

Remember, the Whole Child Parenting Program offers appropriate developmental products and monthly activity books that walk you through supporting your child's skills. Using these in conjunction with the recommended age-appropriate room materials ensures faster development.

ACTIVITY

 Dad and Marcus are in the kitchen; together they are cutting the pizza for the family dinner. Dad asks, "Marcus, would you like to help me cut the pizza?" Marcus replies, "Yes." Dad gives Marcus the pizza cutter. "Marcus, can you tell me what shape the pizza is?" "It is a circle," replies Marcus." Dad then asks, "How do you think we should cut it so all four of us get one piece of pizza?" Marcus replies, "Let's cut it here." He proceeds to cut on the corner of the pizza.

INSIGHT

In this example Dad engages in simple math talk with Marcus. He uses the math words *shape* and *four* and *one*. By Dad giving time for Marcus to respond to the questions, he is giving Marcus an opportunity to look at the pizza and think about how he will cut it into pieces for everyone. Marcus may not be able to correctly cut the pizza into four equal parts, but Dad can help him figure that out.

"Marcus, would you like to help me cut the pizza?"

Over the course of the next week focus on intentionally doing at least three of the following math routines with your child.

1. Lay out your child's outfit for the day on his bed. Ask your child to first put on his undergarments, and then have him count how many pieces of clothing are left on the bed. Next ask your child to put on his pants, and count how many pieces of clothing are left on the bed. Keep going till he is all dressed. This is providing an opportunity for your child to work with subtraction in a simple, age-appropriate way.

2. Before dinner ask your child to set out the napkins on the table. As he sets out each napkin have him count by saying, "One napkin, two napkins, three napkins, four napkins . . ." This is giving your child an opportunity to learn addition.

3. Give your child a banana or apple for afternoon snack. Cut the piece of fruit in half while he watches you, then ask him to put the fruit back together. Let him demonstrate his ability first by watching, then give verbal cues (perhaps by saying "two halves") and contextual cues such as indicating where the pieces might fit together. This is giving your child an opportunity to play with the concepts of *parts* and *whole*.

4. After dinner, have a frozen treat for dessert. Ask your child to count how many people are at the table, and then have him count how many treats he needs so everybody gets one. This will give your child an opportunity to listen to math language (*how many*).

Spatial Relationships >
Spatial Concepts

Spatial concepts define the relationship between your child and objects, as well as the relationship of objects to each other.

ACTIVITY

 Genevieve sits at her table drawing a picture of her family. She starts by drawing a circle the size of a quarter at the top right hand corner of the paper; she puts one larger circle (the size of her palm) under the smaller circle, and then adds straight lines to represent arms, legs, and a body. Genevieve uses smaller circles to draw eyes and a mouth inside the larger circle.

Genevieve repeats this same process to draw four additional forms. Each form is larger than the next, each form is placed on different parts of the paper, and one of the forms is on top of another that is missing legs. The beautiful part about this picture is Genevieve's ability to draw shapes (circles) for objects/forms, show her understanding of spatial relationships in how the forms are placed on the paper (by making use of the entire piece of paper), and making sure everything is inside the paper (nothing drawn off the side).

INSIGHT

As Genevieve grows older and continues to develop her spatial skills she will begin to draw pictures with distinct heads, arms, and torsos. Each shape will start at the bottom of the page (as opposed to the middle of the page); additional objects will be added to the paper to create a complete picture (sun, clouds). As your child develops strong spatial intelligence, she will draw amazing figures, drawings, and paintings. Four year olds are truly dynamic and will always enjoy tools for sketching (e.g. pens, pencils, paint boxes, and drawing paper) as gifts. Take the time to pay attention to your child's drawings. See what you can learn about her spatial development. Make comments to her about where her objects are on the page.

Spatial thinking is very important because as your child becomes aware of the world around her, and the objects that make up her environment, she will show this in her drawings. The objects your child draws will rarely be drawn in connection to one another (where they are drawn on the page). Nor will the drawing be organized on the paper. An example of this is when you look at your child's drawing and see everything "floating" on the paper.

When you see this, your immediate thought is that the picture is wrong, people and objects/forms don't float in space. Don't focus on the product, rather focus on the process your child went through to show you her ability to arrange the objects/forms on the page.

Specific kinds of play are associated with development of certain cognitive skills. Spatial play will support your child's ability to discern where she is in relation to an object and where objects are in relation to other objects.

Parents should support their children's development of spatial skills as early as the age of two, but let's say for a moment you were not thinking about this when your child was two. It is not too late to start teaching the concept because now that your child is four she will be able to grasp the concept of spatial skills more quickly.

And there are fun ways to practice!

Turn an everyday routine into a spatial activity for your child:

1. Talk about things your child can see in a modified version of I Spy, as in "I spy a pink cup in the kitchen on the counter next to the stove" and then have her go find the pink cup.

2. Hide an object that is of interest to your child and then give instruction for her to find it, e.g. "The doll is in the toy chest in the playroom."

3. Ask your child to tell you which things are closer or farther away, e.g. "Which is closer to you: the couch or the TV?"

4. Sit together and complete a 3-D jigsaw puzzle.

5. Build a model together that has detailed instructions and pictures showing how to complete it.

Problem Solving >
Life's Challenges

Problem solving refers to your child's ability to use the knowledge and information she has already acquired to find answers to difficult or complicated issues.

ACTIVITY

Melissa and her brother Robert are thinking about how they will both use the electronic tablet as they sit on the floor, each one wanting a turn at the same time. On this particular day the bickering is louder than usual, and Mom can hear each of them in her room.

Mom comes out of the room and asks, "What are you two so upset about?" Each one explains that the other was not sharing the tablet. Mom asks, "Who used the tablet last? Melissa, I see the tablet in your hand. Did you just have a turn?" Melissa says, "No, I just got the tablet." Mom turns to Robert and says, "Tell your sister you'd like a turn when she is finished. She has ten minutes. I will set the timer." Mom then asks Robert what he would like to do while he is waiting for a turn on the tablet.

INSIGHT

Challenges and frustrations are inevitable, but you have the ability to support your child by giving him problem-solving skills. Mom helps her children solve the problem with the tablet by first identifying the problem (both want a turn using it), giving them an option for a solution (wait ten minutes for the timer to go off), and asking what activity they might engage in to make waiting less difficult. The strategy Mom uses will help the children think about different ways to solve problems of sharing and waiting. Mom is also teaching her children cooperation skills, which are necessary in life for engaging in social interactions.

Your child's ability to learn problem-solving skills is a significant contributor to his social-emotional wellness or self-esteem. Problem-solving skills will empower your child to think about himself and others and what roles he plays. In order to problem solve, your child needs support from you in learning to apply the five-step process of problem solving in every difficult situation that occurs. Remember, the more you practice this process with your child the easier he will learn it until it happens naturally (between ages nine and ten.)

The five steps of effective problem solving:

1. Calm down.
2. Identify the problem.
3. Brainstorm an alternative.
4. Choose a solution.
5. Determine if the solution is successful.

First, your child needs support in calming down. This can be done by encouraging your child to walk away from the situation or listen to soft music. Sometimes children need time to calm down by themselves before they are ready to talk and use language to express their emotions.

Follow by helping to identify the problem. Parents can do this by asking questions such as, "How are you feeling right now?" "Do you know why you are so upset?" or "What happened to make you so upset?" Once you have been able to identify the problem together, you can brainstorm alternative ways to solve the problem.

Once your child identifies the problem, he then acts upon the solution and discovers if it was successful. If it is not successful, try one of the other solutions you brainstormed.

By working through this process with your child, you are modeling how he can do it himself. He will likely feel supported. Your attention is always appreciated and beneficial.

Symbolic Play >
Thinking

Symbolic play is a type of thinking in which symbols or internal images (images in your child's mind) are used to represent objects, persons, and events that are not present.

Most symbolizing (using an object to stand for something else) can be observed through your child's ability to use her imagination in make-believe roles (e.g. playing doctor).

Your child's ability to symbolize occurs in gradual steps and is dependent on interaction with other people and objects in her environment. One example of symbolic play could be your child using a large, empty box as a car after visiting a transportation museum.

It is important for your child to have a variety of opportunities to express herself symbolically; this would include encouraging your child to engage in art, drawing, and writing experiences to enhance symbolic thinking. Dramatic play or pretending also supports symbolic thinking. When your child uses symbolic thought, she accesses her memories to recall what she may have seen an object used for before, or how she could take what is seen and use it in a different way.

ACTIVITY

Remy gets home from half-day preschool. Mom asks Remy, "What did you do today at school?" Remy replies, "Nothing!" Mom then asks, "Well, who did you play with? Did you see your friend Tegan?" Remy replies, "We played princess today."

INSIGHT

As Mom asks who Remy played with and how her day was, she is encouraging Remy to think and remember. Asking these questions is very easy to do; however, remembering is on the lowest level of thinking skills. At the same time, remembering is necessary because it builds the foundation for higher cognitive thinking.

Your child can take in, remember, and recall information at this age fairly easily. You want your child to do more than just spit out information she has heard before; you want her to use her thinking skills.

Remembering is one of the areas parents support the most by asking the five W questions (*who, what,*

"Can I pour some tea for you, bear?"

when, *where*, and *why*). By this time you are probably wondering why remembering is discussed with symbolic play. The answer is very simple: **Play improves memory and stimulates your child's brain.** Your child will pay more attention to a task when she can have periods of play without direction from you. When you give this period of time to your child it supports her capacity to think about play; to plan what will happen; what actions, language, emotional expressions will be given to a specific character your child will play; and what real, symbolic, or invented objects she will use during play. Symbolic play supports this entire process.

ACTIVITY

While sitting at her little table, Lea says to herself out loud, "We have to find something to do until the food is ready. Let's pretend we are going to a tea party." Lea gathers her teacups and places a stuffed bear in the chair. "Can I pour some tea for you, bear?" she asks. "Okay, here you go," she informs the bear. "I just poured your tea. It is hot so blow like this." As Lea pretends to do this with one of the bears, Mom watches from the bedroom door in silence.

INSIGHT

In this example Lea is planning what she is going to do, carrying out her plan, and then recalling what she did. Lea is developing key cognitive skills such as working memory, self-regulation (e.g. being aware of and controlling her feelings and actions), internal language or "self-talk," and the ability to organize, focus, plan, strategize, prioritize, initiate, and perform other skills that will determine her success in school later on. Pretend play helps your child develop these abilities.

2. Social-Emotional Development

> **Social-emotional development is vital because it creates a foundation for lifelong learning; it is related to later academic success and prevents future social and behavioral problems.**

During the preschool years, social-emotional development is about socialization, which is the process by which your child learns values and behaviors accepted by society. It is important to support social skills and your child's ability to control emotions with others. Development in this area leads to school readiness by teaching your child self-regulation, cooperation, and how to develop relationships with others. This skill also allows your child to develop a positive sense of self and sense of his place within the family and community.

WHOLE CHILD: AGE FOUR
Social-Emotional
Development Components

1. Social Development

Social development at this age reflects how your child develops the skills needed to make and keep a friend, cooperate with others, and participate in group activities, which in turn supports school success.

2. Emotional Development

At four, your child has better control of her emotions and has a better understanding of her feelings and what causes those feelings. Having a better understanding of why and how certain feelings come about gives your child the opportunity to problem solve and handle emotions such as anger and sadness. You will also see your four year old picking up on emotional cues when it comes to activities that make her happy and excited. Adults play an important role in helping a child discover her interests and pursue activities that make her happy, thus building her self-esteem.

3. Self-Regulation

Self-regulation is the ability of a child to recognize her own emotions and behaviors. By age four, she has enough language to begin using speaking and listening skills to solve social problems; however, this is also the age when her behavior tends to become more aggressive and more issues with aggression tend to manifest.

4. Self-Awareness

Your child is developing a sense of self through attributes she considers important such as her appearance or the ability to perform certain skills like throwing a ball. Four year olds become aware of their peers' abilities and appearances, too, and will begin to see differences between themselves and others. Your child will continue to build her independence as she sees herself as a person separate from others.

Learning how to appropriately express emotion in social settings is one of the most important social-emotional skills.

Remember, the Whole Child Parenting Program offers appropriate developmental products and monthly activity books that walk you through supporting your child's skills. Using these in conjunction with the recommended age-appropriate room materials ensures faster development.

Social Development >
Friendships

Social development involves your child's ability to learn how to communicate better with others, make connections with peers, resolve conflicts, and gain confidence in her abilities and herself.

Building a strong social foundation is key to your child's happiness because it enables her to better handle stress ("Don't give up!") and keeps her pushing through difficult situations to a satisfactory conclusion ("I did it!").

Characteristics your child will display when she is on the path to satisfying social development:

* mastering basic interaction skills (e.g. smiling, making eye contact, and listening),

* independently approaching other adults and children,

* sharing her feelings with others (can be as simple as mentioning likes and dislikes),

* communicating needs and ideas.

Social development is also defined by culture. What is considered acceptable social behavior in your family, community, or culture may not apply to others. Given the amount of cultural diversity in our world, determining a set social behavioral practice is impossible. Therefore, parents should work toward helping their children learn behaviors that will help them become successful in their school and their environments. By doing so, parents teach their children to respect and value other cultures.

It is important for you to take time to teach your child to be pro-social by doing the following: Teach your child social skills in settings where the skill will be used. For example, when your child arrives at a neighbor's house for a play date make sure she lifts her head, looks into the other parent's eyes, and says hello in a loud, clear voice. If teaching is not possible in a natural setting then engage in a dramatic play experience and role-playing.

Teach social skills that are valued in a natural setting. For example, peers and parents value when your child is polite, uses phrases like "excuse me" when interrupting a conversation, or thanks someone appropriately.

Teach social skills consistently. Teaching must be done several times a day, using simple language, and reinforcing skills in different situations. Since you have your child use manners with others in their environment, make sure she is using manners at home with you. Often children can be more relaxed in their behavior at home and not be so polite. When you teach your child social skills in a proactive way, you will have better success in the skill being used on a continuous basis.

Be highly motivated to improve your child's social skills because social skills problems lead to peer rejection and this can be devastating to your child.

Being a four year old is tough, and being a parent is equally as hard. When children are expected to have good social skills, it will improve behavior and attachments to others. Social skills build trust in others, which supports taking risks to do activities with friends and know that she will be accepted and can accept others.

Emotional Development >
Feelings

It is important for you to look for emotional cues from your child so that you can support her in understanding her emotions.

ACTIVITY

 Lucy and Krish begin to argue about which one of them should have the next turn with the Dr. Seuss book. Lucy begins to cry. Dad comes over and says, "Lucy and Krish, let's take a deep breath together and talk this out. I am here to help you."

INSIGHT

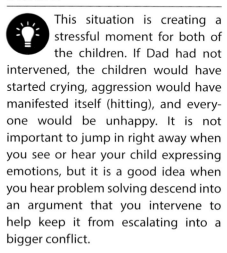 This situation is creating a stressful moment for both of the children. If Dad had not intervened, the children would have started crying, aggression would have manifested itself (hitting), and everyone would be unhappy. It is not important to jump in right away when you see or hear your child expressing emotions, but it is a good idea when you hear problem solving descend into an argument that you intervene to help keep it from escalating into a bigger conflict.

Emotional development involves your child's ability to control emotions, express verbally how she feels, have positive self-esteem, and feel that she can accomplish any task she sets her mind to.

Emotional well-being involves a child's ability to understand the value of her emotions and what causes them. Having emotional well-being will enable your child to build happiness and self-esteem as well as coping abilities for emotions such as anger and sadness. Without strong emotional well-being your child will experience rejection, depression, mood swings, anxiety, and lack of appetite, and poor relationships will be formed.

Encourage your child to use more complex language to express her understanding of feelings and their causes (e.g. your child should say, "I want to try riding on that, but I'm scared.")

Stress plays a big role in your child's emotional development. When your child is always worried, anxious, scared, or unhappy, it affects her health and interactions with others.

Interact with your child affectionately, show consideration for her feelings, and express pride in her accomplishments. Give support in times of stress!

Relationships play a central role in fostering your child's emotions of joy, fear, and anger. When your child has good emotional health, she feels good about herself and is better able to handle stress and engage in relationships. You play an important role in the emotional wellness of your child by providing support as she learns to control her emotions and form good relationships with family, friends, and community. Do one of the following activities with your child at home to build your relationship:

1. Get into her space.
Your child spends a lot of time on the floor. You should be down there, too—playing games, pretending with dolls, building block forts. Work through your feelings of embarrassment and meet with your kids at their level. You might be surprised how fun it can be.

2. Enjoy family time.
Connect with your child by eating together as a family. This is a daily routine and is easy to do, even if it is just for 15 minutes. Talk about the day and how she felt about her day.

3. Do projects together.
Do a family project like cleaning up the garage or collecting recycling materials around the home. At this age you have a child who can and wants to be involved; you don't have to do it all alone.

When you do things as a family and build a strong relationship with your child, this enables you to take time to really learn to read your child's emotional cues so that you can help her identify her emotions. This can only occur when you stop what you're doing, *listen*, and participate!

Self-Regulation >
Self-Control

Self-regulation means
children taking what they
experience and turning it into
information they can use to
control thoughts, emotions,
desires, and behaviors.

ACTIVITY

 Lizzie loves sweets! Mom has just made a batch of chocolate chip cookies; she can smell them all through the house. Lizzie runs to the kitchen and says, "Yum, cookies! I want a cookie, please. Cookies!" Mom replies, "Honey, you will have to wait for them to cool. They are right out of the oven." Lizzie sighs and decides to sit down at the kitchen table while waiting.

Mom hears the baby cry and has to leave the kitchen. Lizzie sits a few minutes more then gets up and walks over to the counter where the cookies are. She looks at them again, stretches out her arm, and opens her hand ... Mom comes back in with the baby.

INSIGHT

Many children love sweets. Try this activity with your child. Leave your child's favorite sweet treat on the kitchen counter. Tell her not to eat it until you return (she has no idea when you will return). See how long it takes before she devours it. This will give you a baseline to see how much self-control your child has.

Self-regulation starts in infancy; some children regulate arousals and sensory motor responses by sucking their thumb when they hear a loud noise. When your child was a toddler, she started complying with your requests.

Now at age four, your child is showing more complex self-regulation skills. For instance, your child will clap after she sees you put on a silly show, but she will not clap while you are giving directions. Self-regulation skills develop gradually over time.

Parents of four year olds can see firsthand how difficult exhibiting self-control can be by witnessing how four year olds push limits. This can be frustrating for you, especially when you are told by pediatricians to make sure you repeatedly and consistently set clear limits.

However, when you state limits repeatedly and then hover over your child to follow through, this will not support her ability to learn self-control. It just creates a situation in which you and your child go back and forth, ultimately ending with her crying and you raising your voice.

Try walking away when your child loses control and see what happens. When your child loses the audience, she tends to calm down. Return later and ask your child if she would like to talk about what just happened.

You play a critical role in shaping your child's self-control. You want your child to learn through you and not through lecturing and attempts to persuade or bribe. Remember, parents must model self-control and not expect it to come naturally for children. It is a skill that can take well into adulthood to master.

Modeling can take place in the following ways:

1. Include your child in decision making (e.g. food choices and what clothing to wear).

2. Offer your child periods of uninterrupted play.

3. Engage in conversations with your child about situations that happened with friends (e.g. sharing toys).

4. Help your child name her emotions and give her suggestions of ways she can calm down independently (e.g. listen to music, look through a book, engage in art).

Self-Awareness >
Self-Identity

Self-awareness refers to your child's sense of self that is retained over time and is based on various attributes he considers important.

For example, "I am the strongest, fastest boy in school." This is a statement by your child that demonstrates his sense of self based on attributes that he considers important (strength and speed). Parents help their child form healthy or unhealthy self-identity concepts of self. Identities in four year olds are encouraged by the parents and environment. For example, you could say to your child, "You are really smart," letting him know what you think about him (self-identity also comes from how he thinks others perceive him). Or you could give a negative image to your child, e.g. giving him the idea that he does not say anything that matters to you. You either increase his intelligence or increase his so-called incompetence. The road you take will help form his self-identity.

Four years old is a critical time for helping your child develop positive self-awareness and a sense of self-esteem. Achieving these goes well beyond making books about themselves, labeling body parts, and stating reasons why he is special or what makes him different.

Self-awareness is a cognitive capacity that initiates a specific step in self-development. Your child's capacity for self-awareness sets the stage for self-conscious social emotions such as embarrassment, pride, and shame that come from your child comparing himself to others.

ACTIVITY

 Allie stands in the mirror looking at her face; she notices she has some hair on the side of her face near her ear. Allie calls for her mom and asks why she has hair on her face. Mom replies, "Some children have facial hair and others do not, and those differences are what make you who you are."

Allie is beginning to see different features about herself that she has never noticed before. Mom supports Allie by building her self-esteem and letting her know everyone looks different and has unique and special features.

INSIGHT

Encouraging self-awareness and self-identification means giving your child's positive self-esteem a boost by showing her how her differences support what it means to have an identity. The self is now recognized not only from a first-person perspective, but also from another person's viewpoint.

Self-awareness starts before your child has strong language development, as seen when she is a toddler and points to her body parts as she looks in the mirror. Your child is evaluating herself against what is perceived by those around her when she shows embarrassment and other painful emotions in a social setting.

Even at this age, your child does not have a full grasp of self-awareness because this is a gradually developed skill and develops continuously. Until your child has a definite conception of self as an independent person, she cannot understand the relationship she has to the surrounding world and thus cannot fully develop self-awareness. As your child matures, however, she will learn more and more about who she is. This learning process continues well into adulthood.

3. Language Development

> **Language development is the process by which four year olds produce sounds, put words together to convey meaning, and communicate.**

It is suggested that language development occurs before children are born, that as fetuses they were able to identify the speech and sound patterns of their mothers. This is why doctors suggest that mothers talk to their babies while in utero. At four months, your child was able to discriminate sound and even read lips; now she is able to make full sentences and invent her own language. There is nothing more remarkable than the emergence of language because it occurs so quickly and is so obvious in a child's interactions with others.

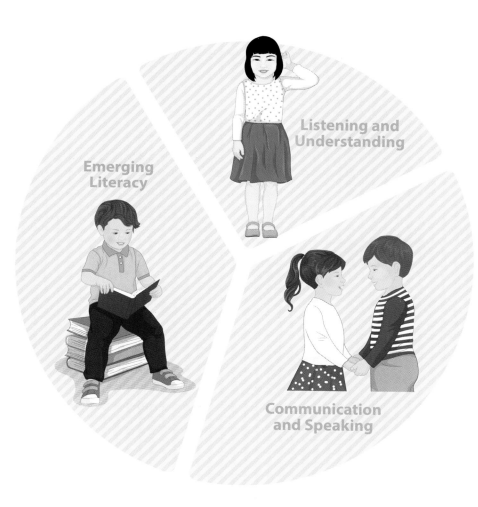

Listening and Understanding

Emerging Literacy

Communication and Speaking

WHOLE CHILD: AGE FOUR
Language
Development Components

Parents facilitate language development in their children through imitation and reinforcement. How parents interact with their children through language develops their children's language skills. Therefore, it is critical to always have language interactions and support children in developing their language skills as proficiency will lead to lifelong academic success.

1.
Listening and Understanding

Listening occurs when your child tunes in to what he can hear and pays attention carefully. By listening, your child learns to hear the differences between sounds, which is a precursor to reading and writing. **Understanding** is how your child makes sense of spoken language, beginning with simple, short sentences and building up to more complex sentences.

2.
Communication and Speaking

Speaking is how your child uses words to express his needs, ideas, and feelings and share what he is thinking with those around him. Four year olds need lots of opportunities to talk and **communicate** before they can start writing.

3.
Emerging Literacy

Emergent or **emerging literacy** is how four year olds interact with books and develop the foundations necessary for learning to read and write. This is an area that uses sensory motor skills because your child will use his vision skills and fine motor skills to form letters and interact with print.

Soon your four year old will begin to start reading and writing if he has not already begun.

Remember, the Whole Child Parenting Program offers appropriate developmental products and monthly activity books that walk you through supporting your child's skills. Using these in conjunction with the recommended age-appropriate room materials ensures faster development.

Listening and Understanding >

I Understand

With listening and understanding come attention skills. Four year olds' ability to focus their attention is a developmental stage vital to the entire process of acquiring language.

ACTIVITY

Camille goes to the public library with her older brother. As she goes off to look at books she sits and listens to the story *The Princess and the Pea*. As the librarian reads the story to the children, she speaks in an animated voice, using high-pitched and low-pitched tones. She also uses props to catch the children's attention. When the story is over, Camille goes over to her brother and excitedly tells him about the story she just heard.

INSIGHT

Camille demonstrates her listening skills by sitting while the librarian is reading. The librarian's use of props enables Camille to focus and gain a better understanding of what the story is about as well as entertaining her. Developing language skills using play and entertainment makes learning fun.

Parents can provide a variety of opportunities for their children to focus their attention and listen carefully. This skill will support all aspects of learning and development, including emerging literacy skills such as phonetic and phonemic awareness, which lead to reading and writing.

When your child was two, she listened with interest when you read stories to her and encouraged her to respond to familiar sounds. At ages three and four, you encourage your child to listen one-on-one or in a small group, such as going to a reading at the bookstore, because she can focus her attention and listen, which leads to understanding.

As your child continues to develop listening skills, you will see improvement in her speaking skills. Your child will say all speech sounds in words. Mistakes will be made with the more difficult sounds, such as "l," "s," "r," and "v," but this is not a cause for alarm.

She will talk without repeating words; name letters and numbers; use sentences that have more than one action word, such as *play* and *jump*; tell a short story; and—best of all—keep the conversation going. It is critical to build your child's vocabulary.

Model listening skills by making sure you are truly listening. Playing games such as Stop, Look, and Listen will encourage your child to pause and pay attention to what she hears.

Give definitions for new words, and use them in sentences: "A taxi is a type of transportation. It is a car. A double decker bus is another type of transportation. So are motorcycles and bicycles."

Understanding involves the way your child comprehends meaning and her interpretation of instructions and problems given to her. Parents will often ask their four year olds, "What did I ask you to do?" When parents do this, they are asking their children to explain what they heard in order to make sure the children understood the directions given to them so the task can be performed.

ACTIVITY

Tanni's neighbor comes over to play. Mom comes in the bedroom and says to Tanni, "When your friend leaves, you need to clean your room and put the dirty clothes in the laundry." At the time, Tanni is so busy playing that Mom is not sure if Tanni has been listening or even has a clear understanding of what she is supposed to do. When Tanni's friend leaves, Mom asks Tanni to come to the room. "Tanni, did you hear what I asked you to do? Please tell me what you are supposed to be doing now that your friend has left." Tanni begins to tell Mom she is supposed to clean her room.

"Please tell me what you are supposed to be doing now."

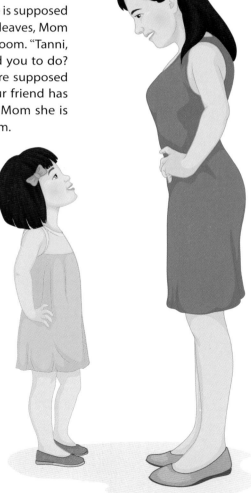

INSIGHT

It is very important for Mom to take the extra step to see if Tanni has listened to her and understands what she is supposed to do. When you do this type of follow up with your child, it encourages her to stop, think, and make meaning out of what she hears. Children need practice more than simply following directions; they need help practicing attending to oral language and interpreting what they hear. So give your child many opportunities to listen carefully to specific requests you have each day.

Your child has the ability to retell a story she has heard or create a story using a wordless picture book.

In a storytelling event, your child has not memorized the words; rather, she is interpreting and paraphrasing the words as she understands them through a spontaneous performance, assisted by audience interaction. For children to retell stories, they must understand what they heard.

They are able to understand the main idea of the story, recognize the characters, and organize the facts.

Understanding is important to your child's ability to build her language and literacy skills because it is also a necessary cognitive skill used in storytelling.

Stories provide a four year old with the mental framework for thinking so she can shape experiences into a whole that she understands. Storytelling allows your child to mentally map experiences and see pictures in her head; it gives her a model of language and thought she can imitate. Remembering and understanding occurs when your child answers questions that require her to organize previously gleaned information.

It is important for parents to create an environment that is rich in language opportunities for their children.

Communication and Speaking >
I Said That?

Language development incorporates an ever-growing vocabulary. Four year olds will understand how sounds and words can be married to create sentences and communicate with others.

ACTIVITY

Robert goes to the park with his older sister. At the park he gets really excited because in the distance he sees something really big. He cannot figure it out at first. Robert says to his sister, "A bear! I see a bear on the grass, by the tree!" His sister looks up and says, "Oh Robert, it's a deer not a bear. We don't have bears here!"

When Robert arrives back home, he runs into the living room where his mom and dad are sitting. Robert says, "Guess what? I saw a bear at the park! Oh, no, not a bear. What did we see?" His sister replies, "A deer." Robert says, "Yes, I saw a deer, and it was huge like the size of a bear!"

INSIGHT

Robert comes home and tells a short story about his experience during the day. He demonstrates his ability to communicate using descriptive words (*huge*) and complete sentences; he even uses connecting words (*by* the tree).

A rich language environment has an essential impact on the rapid development of your child's cognitive abilities (brain development). Communication and language support personal, social, and emotional development because your four year old can communicate feelings, needs, and ideas, as well as develop a strong sense of self-awareness.

At four, your child uses more than 1,500 different words, knows about 4,000 words, and understands even more. Words four year olds speak and understand fall into four categories:

1. **Connecting words, such as *when* and *but***—"When I grow up, I am going to play soccer."

2. **Words that explain emotions, such as *upset* and *angry***—"I am angry at you."

3. **Words that explain something that is on his mind, such as *remember***—"Remember, Mom took us to the park? We played on the rocket slide."

4. **Words that explain where things are, such as *on top of* and *below***— "The cat is on top of the car."

Connecting words come from your child's increased language development. He now has the ability to connect words and make a sentence or statement using those words.

Emotion words come from your four year old's social-emotional development. Your four year old is showing you how he uses words to express feelings as opposed to acting out those feelings.

Words about things on his mind come from having a better understanding of what he recalls and how well he can remember events from the past.

Using words about where objects or people are shows your four year old's growth in spatial development and his ability to see the location of objects around him.

Retell Stories

For your child to retell stories, he must tap into his creative and imaginative skillsets to recreate the story.

Children are taking everything that they have learned in the past and applying it to present skills they are developing, which prepares them for learning new skills in the future.

Remember to give yourself praise and encouragement for supporting your child's language growth.

A child's growth in language is one of the most obvious manifestations of cognitive development, and it provides great joy to parents as they watch it progress.

Emergent Literacy >
Learning to Read and Write

Emerging or emergent literacy development describes how children acquire reading and writing skills.

Language, reading, and writing are linked together, and they develop together continuously through the use of literacy materials. Literacy materials are things such as magazines, books, newspapers, crayons, and markers.

Everything your child has done at previous ages, from gumming a book to singing nursery rhymes, has paved the way for literacy development. Language and literacy skills are learned best when four year olds can enjoy books independently and interact with other children and adults, as well as through literacy rich experiences provided by you.

Printed words, in storybooks or in the environment, allow children to connect themselves to faraway places. Exposure to books and print, as well as having conversations that prompt children to discuss the people and important events in their lives, encourages children to discover that written words are another way to share ideas. It is important to practice literacy skills every day with your four year old by making literacy a part of your routine. Have your four year old repeat a simple story after you read it.

ACTIVITY

 Patty is reading a book with her niece. Patty reads, "It was a dark and stormy—" and then stops reading. Patty asks her niece, "What comes next?"

INSIGHT

 By asking this question, Patty is helping her niece make simple predictions about the story being read to her. This helps her develop literacy skills.

Some children are starting to recognize different letters, especially ones in their name; they can connect a letter with the sound it makes and understand that these sounds make up words. Some can already "read" common words they see, like the word *stop* on the sign at the corner.

ACTIVITY

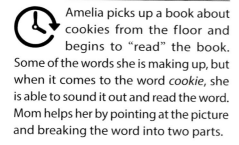 Amelia picks up a book about cookies from the floor and begins to "read" the book. Some of the words she is making up, but when it comes to the word *cookie*, she is able to sound it out and read the word. Mom helps her by pointing at the picture and breaking the word into two parts.

INSIGHT

Amelia is demonstrating emerging literacy skills. She can recognize certain words that are important to her. By giving her contextual cues and breaking the word into parts, Mom is supporting her child's largely independent efforts.

Once your child understands and recognizes more words in print, you will find that she loves to play games with words. She wants to have fun with literacy. So join in with her. Read a book and then play act the characters. Using only the pictures in a book make up the story yourselves. Dress up like the characters in a book and write down a new story about them. Literacy skill building can be lots of fun.

ACTIVITY

 Mona's mom wants to play a reading game called What Can You Read? Mom writes names of objects around the house (e.g. *window*, *sink*, *mirror*, *rail*, etc.) on paper and tapes the words next to the object. Mom says, "Mona, let's play What Can You Read? Go around and find all the words and read them out loud. The ones you can't read we will do together."

INSIGHT

Because Mom puts the labels next to the objects, she supports her daughter's early literacy skills. Offering to help keeps the activity from becoming overwhelming or boring.

Earlier we discussed how reading, writing, and language develop together. In Mona's game What Can You Read? Mom can extend the learning further to include writing skills. Since your four year old is developing more control over her hands and fingers, she can use literacy materials like pencils. Remember that she is still learning to write letters, so let your child practice with pencils and paper as often as possible.

In this example, after all the words are collected from Mona's What Can You Read? game, Mom asks Mona to pick two of the words she wants to learn to write. Mona picks *box* and *cup*. Mom gives Mona a thin piece of paper to put on top of the card and has Mona trace the letters. When Mona gets the hang of "writing" letters this way, Mom can then provide lined paper.

Sit down with your child and have her help you make the shopping list. This activity will support literacy development through writing. It will also get her more involved in making healthful food choices!

Sight Words

Sight words are very important on the path of teaching your child to read. This is a perfect time for parents to learn more about Dolch sight words. Dolch sight words are words that have been identified as high frequency words that will be used starting at the age of four and carry through to seven or eight years of age. These words occur in about 75% of the books and materials children see and need to be learned by memory, regardless of where the child is in phonetical learning. Some of these common sight words include:

all   and   hot   how   let   not   man   may   dry   eat
fly   off   our   put   red   sit   some   the   mom

You can find more sight words below specific to this age and create a sight word wall in your home. Once a week together pick a sight word, tape it on your refrigerator, and try to work on using the word in conversations you have with each other at home.

not   one   and   can   for   see   big   red   you   the   run

One thing you may have noticed is that all of these words consist of three letters. Four-letter sight words can be learned after your child masters three-letter sight words. This does not mean your child can only learn to read three-letter words, but it is easier to start off small and build up in complexity.

These words are also good to start with when your child is learning to write. When you use sight words combined with writing, you can also teach the sounds that are associated with each letter. This will support reading and writing development.

Practice reading and writing skills by making a name card for your child. Place it next to things that belong just to your child (e.g. her coat or lunchbox). Make the card colorful and clear. Show your child that the letters spell an important word: her own name.

Teaching Your Child to Read

Many parents are very excited to start teaching their children to read, but some groundwork must first be laid. Your child needs to know the differences between pictures and print, understand how books are read (from left to right), and see the differences between uppercase and lowercase letters.

Your child can start identifying most letters between the ages of four and five, so now is a great time to start teaching her the alphabet and letter sounds. Parents can then start teaching their children how to pick out and differentiate between individual letter sounds, which is called **phoneme isolation**. Children who are exposed to more print and text at home tend to make these connections sooner.

There are a number of different ways you can teach your child letter sounds. Start with the your child's name and sound out each letter by having her clap her hands as she says her name. This can be done with any word; over time, children will grasp this concept of words being broken down into separate sounds and syllables. Once she learns her name phonetically and by spelling it out, go back to the alphabet.

Introduce two letters a week. Pick letters that are important to your child. If she is focused on space, use the letters S and P. Introduce one letter at a time by pointing out things in the house that start with that letter. Say the sound that the letter makes then say the name of the letter: PUH, P. You can even take turns going through the alphabet using the sounds of the letters instead of the names of the letters: AH, BUH, KUH, DUH, etc.

By following these steps, you will help your child start reading, which leads to writing.

Teaching your child to read will take more time for some children and less for others. Patience and practice are the keys to success!

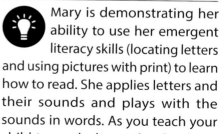

Mary is demonstrating her ability to use her emergent literacy skills (locating letters and using pictures with print) to learn how to read. She applies letters and their sounds and plays with the sounds in words. As you teach your child to read, choose books about subjects that'll really catch her interest or make her laugh. One of the keys to improving literacy is to keep reading stories to your child; this improves concentration and imagination, particularly once you progress beyond basic picture books. Reading aloud is crucial to nurturing the love of reading.

ACTIVITY

Mary is standing in the living room and takes a book from the shelf. It is a book that is very familiar to her, *The Little Kittens*. Mary begins to say, "One." Mary then flips to the next page and says, "A, and." As Mary looks through the book she points out familiar letters and pictures on the pages.

4. Creative Development

> **The right side of the brain is best at expressive and creative tasks. Creativity is both a skillset and a distinct and individual personality system that is developed throughout a child's life and refined in adolescence and adulthood.**

Positive creative experiences are needed along your child's educational journey. When you support your child's creativity, you boost her confidence and ability to express her ideas using visual symbols, and you increase her learning potential. Creative thinking and the ability to show meaning in many ways are the keys to success in the 21st century.

Creativity experiences boost your child's learning and development in several ways. Some of the ways include cognitive problem solving, self-regulation, and the development of tools for communication and meaning making. In order to provide quality creative experiences for your child you need to give her different mediums to create art. For example, you should offer your child a brush to paint with, but also tools like rollers and sponges so she can create a contemporary painting. Children love to draw; offer your child crayons, but also colored chalks and oil pastels. Your child has ideas; continue to encourage her to be imaginative and creative!

Dramatic Play

Music

Visual Arts

Dance

WHOLE CHILD: AGE FOUR
Creative
Development Components

1. Music

Music, a complex blend of sounds, is created by using the voice or instruments, or a combination of both to make a melody, harmony, and rhythm. The singing voice is the primary instrument your child uses automatically. Parents support their child in music by offering instruments to be used in combination with the voice to extend learning.

2. Dance

Deliberate and intentional movements performed with awareness are what evolve into dance once your child matures. Watch her twirl, whirl, and move her hips side to side in response to music.

3. Visual Arts

Visual art forms include such activities as drawing, painting, sculpture, crafts, and photography. Visual art includes many other artistic endeavors, such as creating textile art; this is when your child creates a picture by gluing different fabric and yarn pieces onto paper or canvas.

4. Dramatic Play

Dramatic play occurs when your child represents her understanding of her experiences through role-playing and imitating, adding language to the mix.

Keeping art materials around and accesible at all times gives your child the opportunity to be creative anytime.

Remember, the Whole Child Parenting Program offers appropriate developmental products and monthly activity books that walk you through supporting your child's skills. Using these in conjunction with the recommended age-appropriate room materials ensures faster development.

Music >
Singing and Playing

It is a wonderful experience to watch your child engage in singing and "playing" an instrument.

Your child is learning music in much the same way she learned language. For example, after listening to the sounds of her native language, she began to babble, experimenting with speech sounds. Soon afterward, she imitated words and used them meaningfully in phrases and sentences.

ACTIVITY

 Sara is playing with her dolls in her bedroom; she says, "I know you're sleepy, dolly. Let's go to sleep now." Sara begins to sing her dolly a lullaby. "Hush, little baby, don't say a word. Mama's gonna buy you a mocking bird, and if that bird won't sing, Mama's gonna buy you a diamond ring. Shh!"

As Sara sings the song she speaks some of it and sings some of it; this results in her losing the pitch and tempo. When Sara places "shh" sounds at the end of the song, she is making reference to being quiet so the dolly can sleep.

INSIGHT

Sara demonstrates she is in the rhythm babble stage of music development; this is indicated by her inability to keep tempo, pitch, or rhythm. This is appropriate, however, because at this stage of development the skill reflects a simple musical experience between Sara and her dolly.

Musical sound is created to express ideas that your child has in her head. She creates music and responds to music.

Your child starts the stage with **music babble**, in which she makes sounds that do not make musical sense. She will move into **tonal babble** next, in which she sings in a speaking voice. In **rhythm babble** she will make voice sounds that are not on tempo. By the time she is four, she has started to be able to sing most of a short song correctly.

Picking up an instrument will help your child express herself and support social development. **She will love to experiment with a variety of instruments with you and other children as she learns to work with others to create sounds.** This enables her to create sound patterns with her instrument, her body, and her voice. Have you observed your child making noises with her armpits? Even though it may not sound like a musical sound, it is your child trying to make sound patterns with her body as the instrument.

This age is a great time to open up your child's musical world by having her take music lessons. You would not start vocal lessons because your child is not at that stage of development. You could start her on an instrument as she is developing fine motor (small muscle) skills at a rapid pace.

Picking an instrument for your child is exciting; often parents pick something they wished they knew how to play; however, it is more important to pick an instrument based on your child's personality. Below are some instruments to think about.

1. **Does your child like being the center of attention?**
   Flutes are great; many musical compositions contain flute solos.

2. **Is your child outgoing?**
   Saxophones and trumpets are good as they are lead instruments.

3. **Do you have a petite child?**
   Bassoons are ideal for small children.

4. **Does your child have large hands or long fingers?**
   Pianos are a desirable choice.

Whatever instrument you choose for your child, when you choose one that suits her personality you create a more supportive experience that is set up for long-term success.

Expose your child to different instruments and sounds by listening to music, visiting an instrument store, and watching a live ensemble performance in your community or local civic center.

Dance >
Boogie and Groove

The words *dance* and *movement* are interchangeable when discussing creative development.

Dance is a form of art, and the human body is the canvas. It is your child's body moving in space and time with energy. Dance is a form of cultural expression; it supports the development of many other abilities.

Dance will teach your child the value of creativity, and the skills of problem solving, risk taking, and higher-order thinking.

Earlier in the book, we discussed how learning one skill leads to learning another skill and that many areas of learning have an effect on another area. This is the same for dance; it helps your child to grow physically, emotionally, socially, and cognitively. Many parents can see how dance enhances their child's physical skills but are less familiar with how dance develops other skills. Let's take a moment and visit two areas.

Social-emotional development: At this age, children want a dance partner or an audience. Dance promotes social interaction and cooperation. Your child will communicate with you through dance and the movements of his body. Dance is an excellent outlet for a four year old to express emotions and feelings. Dancing enables your child to be aware of himself in a particular music-filled space.

More importantly, dance develops the brain and teaches your child to think about the different ways he will move his body. But you have to give him tools to help him be successful with it. Tools include music to listen to and props like scarves and instruments to help support movement and music skills. If you just say to your child, "Dance," but you don't give him tools, he'll just stand there. Four year olds like to discover what their bodies can do. They delight in isolating body parts, changing directions and levels, exploring each part's range of motion, and increasing their abilities.

Dance requires your child to expand his range of motion and use every part of the body. It includes fine motor (small muscle) and gross motor (big muscle) skills, as the body parts are moved in different directions at the same time, hands included. Your child will improve his coordination skills as he learns to twirl around without falling.

A dance-infused environment will lead to new moves and new skills for your child. He will eventually feel a sense of accomplishment at conquering tasks, leading to higher levels of general self-esteem than if he was never to have dance as a part of his life.

Through dance, physical development is expanded in the following ways:

1. Flexibility—Your child can sit and touch his toes with his hands and hold his feet.

2. Stamina—When your child was a toddler he got tired after five minutes of dancing; now your child can engage in a dance experience for 30 to 45 minutes.

3. Posture—As your child learns to stretch his body and keep his shoulders back he will stand straighter and have better posture.

4. Weight—Dance can help a child who is overweight slim down.

Visual Arts >
Images

Visual arts comprise
a vast category that
includes drawing,
craftmaking, collage,
mosaic, photography,
sculpture, and
more.

ACTIVITY

Kayla recently received a box of pastel chalks from her mom. Kayla asks her mom if she can go outside and use her new chalk set. Kayla looks up at the sky, then looks down at the pavement and begins to draw a cloud and a sun with the chalk. She draws the lines on the sun to show that the sign is shining brightly. Kayla calls to her mom, "Look, Mom! I drew the sky!"

INSIGHT

In this experience Kayla creates a picture that is a form of realistic art. Realism has the appearance of a recognizable subject, be it an object, person, or place. When you look at Kayla's art, you can point and say, "Oh, that's a sun and a cloud." Visual art creates and strengthens the neural connections in her brain as she explores the texture of the chalk on the pavement. Kayla's parents have supported her visual art skills by simply providing her with a tool: chalk.

Visual art allows your child to explore the world without having to actually create an art piece herself; this is because visual art can be seen throughout your child's environment (e.g. a sculpture or a fountain).

When your child is able to explore visual art using a variety of different mediums—such as paint, play dough, canvas, oil pants, and watercolors—it enables her to develop both the right and left side of the brain by teaching perceptual, cognitive, and discrimination skills that will aid with reading ability and expand gross motor (large muscle) and fine motor (small muscle) skills!

Parents are role models for their children and the development of their visual art skills. Participate in art with your child and make materials readily accessible. Materials can include some of the mediums discussed above; in addition to these, set up a dedicated space within your home.

When your child creates art, take a moment to discuss her creation together. Talk about the colors that were used. This will provide a supportive environment in which your child can take a moment and reflect on her work.

Create a space to display her work. This will make her feel confident and build her self-esteem.

Engaging in visual arts when your child is young can nurture the creative spirit.

Four year olds who are exposed to a wide variety of arts and crafts are more likely to create unique inventions that are patent worthy, come up with ideas that start companies, or publish papers and books on science and technology. Many problem-solving situations require creative solutions. When you support your child in visual arts, you are supporting her ability to be creative and think "outside the box."

Engaging in creating and appreciating visual arts is both fun and educational.

Dramatic Play >
Pretend Play

Dramatic play, also known as *pretend play*, can be defined as your child using her imagination to come up with ways to role play and portray life experiences.

ACTIVITY

 Lisa is in her bedroom dressed up in her fairy costume. She has her dolls lined up. "Dolly, do you want to make a wish? Yes? Do you want to come fly with me? Okay. I will teach you. Don't be afraid. I am here." Lisa picks up the dolly and "flies" her around the room.

INSIGHT

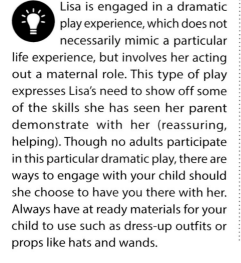 Lisa is engaged in a dramatic play experience, which does not necessarily mimic a particular life experience, but involves her acting out a maternal role. This type of play expresses Lisa's need to show off some of the skills she has seen her parent demonstrate with her (reassuring, helping). Though no adults participate in this particular dramatic play, there are ways to engage with your child should she choose to have you there with her. Always have at ready materials for your child to use such as dress-up outfits or props like hats and wands.

Because the definition of dramatic play is so broad, we have to look at the many ways your child will participate in this experience.

Have you ever noticed your child engaged in a dramatic play experience? This is interesting to watch because you realize just how much listening your child has been doing, e.g. when speaking to her dolls she uses many of the words you use. Or perhaps she uses her transportation toys to act out a construction scene you saw while on a walk in the neighborhood.

Have you ever made the comment to someone, "All my child wants to do is play all day?" Many people have devalued the importance of dramatic play/pretend play because they think that pretending or using symbols that stand in for that which is real is not important for school readiness.

Dramatic play intertwines with all areas of your child's development, including.

Language and literacy build your child's oral skills, which are developing as she has conversations, negotiates, and takes on roles during dramatic play. You can see this as she uses vocal changes with puppetry or makes signs on poster board for her backyard construction site. Parents can support their children in language development through dramatic play by reading aloud stories and providing animation in their voices when using puppets.

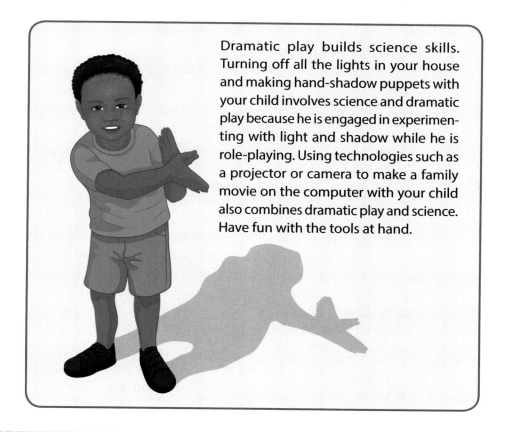

Dramatic play builds science skills. Turning off all the lights in your house and making hand-shadow puppets with your child involves science and dramatic play because he is engaged in experimenting with light and shadow while he is role-playing. Using technologies such as a projector or camera to make a family movie on the computer with your child also combines dramatic play and science. Have fun with the tools at hand.

5. Physical Development

> **Physical development refers to your child's ability to use both gross (large muscle) motor skills and fine (small muscle) motor skills to move his body in different ways and patterns.**

As your child's body becomes sleeker and less top heavy, his center of gravity shifts downward. As a result, balance improves, paving the way for new motor skills involving large muscles of the body. When your child becomes steadier on his feet, his arms and body are freed to experiment with new skills: throwing and catching balls, steering tricycles, and swinging on horizontal bars and rings.

Your child is learning to move in space, move with confidence, and control all of his smaller muscles that move when he picks up something or puts it down. In physical development, children are developing body confidence, which encourages them to push their bodies to try new things, move in new ways, and even challenge themselves to see if they can jump farther or higher than they ever did before.

Physical development also supports the health of your child and helps maintain a healthy lifestyle. This includes the amount of time they spend

WHOLE CHILD: AGE FOUR
Physical
Development Components

moving their bodies versus sitting and watching TV or other passive activities. It includes the types of foods they put in their bodies to give them energy for movement and to gain new physical skills. Physical development also involves the ways in which your child will use a range of small and large muscles to gain new skills.

1. Gross Motor Skills

Gross motor skills are larger movements your child will make with his arms, legs, feet, or his entire body. Gross motor development started in infancy as your child began to sit up (using the torso to stabilize himself) and crawl (using the leg muscles), and it continues to grow as he matures.

2. Fine Motor Skills

Fine motor skills are small movements such as picking up small objects like a marble or toothpick. This area also started developing in infancy as your child learned to hold a spoon or a cup. Small muscles are developed in the fingers, toes, wrists, lips, and tongue.

3. Sensory Motor Skills

Sensory motor development involves children's brains receiving sensory messages and then producing a response that uses fine motor or gross motor skills. This information is received from the body and his environment through what he sees, hears, smells, tastes, and touches, as well as the **vestibular sense** (movement and balance) and **proprioception** (sense of his own body).

At about age four you can start teaching your child how to tie her shoes. Use the "bunny" ears method. And be patient!

Remember, the Whole Child Parenting Program offers appropriate developmental products and monthly activity books that walk you through supporting your child's skills. Using these in conjunction with the recommended age-appropriate room materials ensures faster development.

Gross Motor Skills >
Developing the Large Muscles

Gross motor skills are skills that involve different body parts such as your child's feet, legs, head, and arms.

Put on the sunscreen and take your child outdoors. Encourage him to run at different speeds or toss and catch balls of different sizes. By doing so you support gross motor skill development.

This is also the time when you can put your child in gymnastics, more advanced swimming classes, ballet, soccer, T-ball, or karate. These activities support his gross motor skill development, but there are things a parent can do at home as well. When you go to the park, let your child try to walk along a very low wall. He can walk a two-inch line for at least 10 feet without stepping off if you provide the experience for him to practice.

Play a game of tiptoe around the house or stomp to music. Turn on soft music first and tiptoe as softly as you can. Then play a marching band song and stomp around the house together. Four year olds can tiptoe, which encourages them to learn to balance without their hands held out for support.

Gross motor skills are important for your child to perform everyday functions, such as walking and running. These are critical for every-day self-care skills like dressing because you need to be able to stand on one leg to put on your pants without falling over. Gross motor skills impact the endurance your child needs to cope with a full day of school or home activities. In other words, gross motor skills improve your four year old's muscular strength, endurance, posture, body awareness, balance, co-ordination, and muscle tone. Play with your child and enjoy all the things his body can do.

ACTIVITY

Ross is very excited because today he is going to his very first children's gym class. He sits thinking about what he will do in the class. In gym class the teacher places three hula-hoops in the middle of the floor. "Today, class, we will jump and hop in and out of the hoops. You will need to keep your hands extended at your side to give you balance. Let me show you how," says the teacher. After the teacher shows the children how to hop and jump in and out of the hoops, Ross has a turn. He starts at the nearest hoop, extends his arms, and hops from one hoop to another with alternating feet. "Good job, Ross! You made it to the other side without falling," says the teacher.

INSIGHT

This activity helps Ross develop his gross motor skills as he hops in one hula-hoop and out another. Ross is not only developing his leg muscles, he is also developing his arm muscles as he keeps his arms extended for balance while he hops. Gross motor skills develop very quickly during the early years. Now that your four year old has some confidence in his gross motor abilities, this is the time when you can support him even further. In Ross' case you can support his skills by adding a tunnel at the end of the hoops. Then he works on going from a standing position to a bending and crawling position.

Fine Motor Skills >
Small Muscles

Fine motor development is defined as the development of smaller muscle movement that involves using the hands and fingers to carry out detailed tasks.

You have witnessed first hand how your child has progressed in the area of fine motor development as you watched her go from uncontrolled hand moments in infancy, then bringing objects to her midline (middle of body) and picking up smaller objects as a baby, to using a crayon to scribble and a finger to point as a toddler; and now she can tie her shoe, use scissors, write with a pencil, draw circles on a paper, and "type" on a computer. Fine motor skills enable your child to grasp, hold, and manipulate small objects.

ACTIVITY

Samantha is now four years old. Samantha walks by the office and notices her dad working at his desk writing something. "Dad, can I have a pencil and paper, please?" asks Samantha. She loves to use more refined writing tools such as pencils and pens instead of crayons or markers. Samantha then takes the items and sits at her table. She starts at the top of paper and begins to make a series of zigzag lines on the paper.

INSIGHT

In this scenario Samantha is demonstrating her ability to use her fine motor skills by pretending to write or creating a piece of art. This is a skill that is reflective of a child who is four, because it takes precision to make sharp lines. Fine motor skills play a significant role in your child's physical development because the arms, hands, and fingers work together to complete the task. Fine motor development is ongoing. It never stops. Even as an adult Samantha may continue to refine her fine motor skills by learning to play an instrument or build and paint model airplanes.

Your child was not able to progress through the timeline of fine motor development without having a strong foundation. You gave her this foundation as you provided her with learning experiences to increase hand-eye coordination skills, allowed her to have greater independence as she learned to open drawers and cabinets, and let her participate in routine tasks at home like picking up her clothes. All of these activities helped your child develop finger strength and control.

Fine motor development involves the senses. One in particular is her sense of sight and hand-eye coordination skills using her eyes to control the movements of the muscles of the hands, fingers, and wrists. Just as you supported your child in building the foundation needed to develop fine motor skills, you must continue to support her in refining her fine motor skills with specific activities provided through play experiences.

Parents can draw straight lines on paper and let their children cut along the lines or let them trace over their names if they cannot write the letters independently. Brushing teeth independently encourages fine motor development.

Activities that support small muscle development include your child buttoning her own buttons. If she is unable to do so independently, support her by starting the button and then letting her finish. Show your child how to tie her shoes by modeling side by side or by using the "bunny ear" method.

When your child serves her own food this encourages wrist development, as does pasting pictures on paper. There are many everyday experiences that can be created for your child to hone fine motor skills. Many of the skills once refined will lead to your child developing writing and articulation skills for language development. If your child does not practice her fine motor development skills, she will weaken and lose her ability to perform some tasks required by her hands (e.g. the ability to hold scissors properly or use a pencil). Have you ever heard someone say, "I used to play piano and now I can't?" When you ask what happened the response is usually, "I stopped practicing years ago." A fine motor skill is like this: Without practice and refinement you can severely limit your ability to continue performing the skill.

Fine motor development supports strong writing skills. Strong writing skills will last your child a lifetime!

Sensory Motor Skills >
Movement Makes "Sense"

Sensory motor skills involve getting stimuli from the environment through the senses, which are processed by the brain; the brain then sends the required information for action to the appropriate body part.

ACTIVITY

 Talia joins a soccer program for the summer. Today the girls are practicing kicking the ball; it is Talia's turn to practice kicking. Her coach tells her to line her body up a few feet away from the ball, to look at the ball ahead of her, then approach the ball, and kick.

INSIGHT

This process of telling Talia how to kick the ball may seem unnecessary, but it is a clear example of the steps children use with their sensory motor skills to achieve a motor task.

Early on, we defined sensory motor skills as including the senses; one of those senses is the **vestibular** (movement and balance) sense. It has a huge influence in your child's daily life.

Vestibular sense helps your child keep her balance, provides coordination for movement of her head with her eyes, gives her the ability to use both sides of her body together, and allows her to remain upright against the pull of gravity (like when a strong wind blows). It is a prerequisite skill for whole-body locomotion or movement. For example, being able to stand without falling allows for putting on pants; this motor skill also permits exploration of your child's surrounding space and the objects in it.

When the vestibular sense is working efficiently and effectively in your child, it will free up all the rest of her higher cognitive functioning and motor skills.

Maintaining balance is vitally important because it provides a base on which she can build other physical skills.

ACTIVITY

 Four-year-old Matthew is in the children's book area at the library listening to story hour. The book being read is about dinosaurs, which is a topic Matthew loves. Out of the corner of his eye he sees a play area with dinosaur toys.

Matthew gets up during the story and heads over to the play area. As soon as he gets up and begins to walk he trips over his feet and topples onto the floor.

He picks himself up and goes to play with the other children.

INSIGHT

This scenario demonstrates how some children at this age can have difficulty with their developing vestibular sense.

We see this in the case of Matthew, specifically with his inability to pay attention to the story being read, and the difficulty he encounters with coordination, being clumsy.

This is why it is vitally important for you to help your child develop this sense and thus increase sensory motor abilities.

Below is an example of a specific activity you can do with your child. Start by doing the activity one time a week, then build up to two times a week; continue on a daily basis as you watch your child grow.

Eye movement control exercise
(seeing supports focus, which supports balance)

Many parents have at least one set of blocks at home. Sit with your child and create block designs. To get prepared for this activity, take five or 10 square blocks and arrange them in a shape on a piece of paper. Trace around the outside of the shape. Repeat this process four more times, creating four different block shapes on paper.

Then give your child the paper and his blocks, and ask your child to fit the blocks inside the shape by placing them on the paper. At first you will see your child putting the blocks inside the shape but not paying attention to the lines. This is why it will be important for you to demonstrate one shape and then let him do the rest himself.

It is important that parents help their children develop their use of the senses to support locomotion and navigation in the world around them by continuously providing movement experiences.

It is difficult for your child to integrate multisensory skills for balance and locomotion because his sensory and motor capabilities are still developing. Tasks such as learning to swim may take more time, but that does not mean they should not be attempted.

6. Health and Care

> **Your child's sense of independence is growing, and he is beginning to take his health and care into his own hands.**

He can now excuse himself to go to the potty without being prompted, start to brush his own teeth, and begin to wash his own hair. It is still important to monitor your child to guarantee that his body, teeth, and hair are cleaned well. You can also introduce other hygiene regimens such as flossing. If the doctor has not already, he or she will start talking to you about getting your child ready for school and all the checkpoints (hearing, vision, innoculations and a dental exam) needed for enrollment, as well as how to get your child prepared for this new routine.

Four year olds are more confident with their movement abilities, so they may test their limits more. This can result in scrapes, cuts, or bruises. Remember that the first thing you should do in these bumpy circumstances is stay calm and tend to your child.

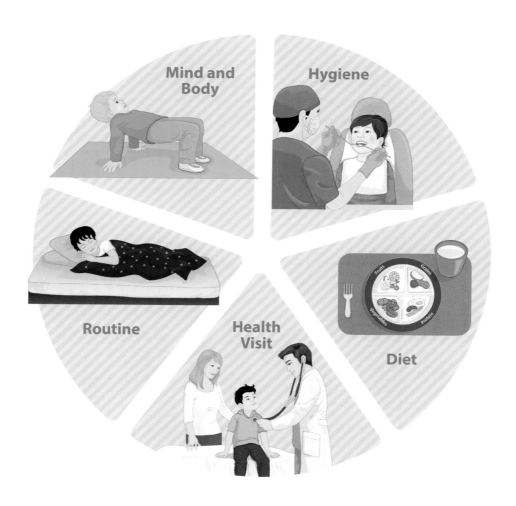

WHOLE CHILD: AGE FOUR

Health and Care

Hygiene >

Your child is capable of understanding not only the reasons for good hygiene, but also what happens when you don't practice good hygiene.

At this age, it is still important to help your child and make sure she washes her hands properly.

Encourage her to sing a song such as "Happy Birthday" or "Twinkle, Twinkle, Little Star" before she rinses the soap off her hands. This makes sure she is washing long enough to get the germs off her hands.

Take advantage of soaps that foam or smell to get your child excited about washing her hands. Make the sink easily accessible for your child; have a stepstool and soap readily available to make it easier for her to be more independent and productive.

Don't use rewards or punishments for your child when it comes to personal hygiene. Explain to her that these are things that are necessary to keep her healthy and safe from illness. Explain that she can't sit down and have snack until she washes her hands or that you can't read a bedtime story until she brushes her teeth.

Oral Care

Your child is more independent and is brushing her teeth every morning and night on her own; however, it is still important to monitor and make sure she is brushing her teeth properly. A good tool to introduce is a timer. There are a variety of digital and manual timers that can make it fun for your child as well as help her brush her teeth for the proper amount of time: two minutes.

Four years old is when your dentist will talk about thumb or finger sucking. It is important to start breaking your child of this habit now. Your pediatrician or dentist is trained to help with this problem, too, so seek advice if needed.

It is important to end this habit because it can start affecting your

child's adult teeth as well as spread germs due to your child's hands being in and out of her mouth after touching surfaces.

Your dentist will also talk to you about the correct amount of fluoride your child needs in her toothpaste at this early age. **Too much fluoride can stain your child's teeth and can also be toxic.** There are supplemental gels and special toothpastes made for children.

Milk contains sugars that are harmful to teeth. Have your child rinse with water after she drinks milk, and don't allow her to drink milk an hour to two hours before bedtime.

Now is the time to introduce floss to your child. Stop for a moment and think about your flossing practices. Do you floss regularly? Most adults do not, and if you don't floss, how can you possibly expect your child to pick up the habit?

According to dentists flossing is even more important than brushing when it comes to preventing disease and tooth decay. This is because brushing only gets the surface of your child's teeth; much food gets lodged between the teeth and decays there.

As with brushing your child will need supervision until she is about seven or eight years of age.

Flossing made simple:

1. Have your child cut off a piece of floss 18 inches long.

2. Have your child wrap the ends around her middle or index fingers on both hands.

3. Have your child gently guide the floss between her teeth, moving the floss around the tooth and under the gum line.

4. Alternatively, there are disposable flossing sticks that children can use for the same effect. They break easily so she may need to use more than one a day.

Talk to your dentist about how to maintain healthy gums and lessen the occurrence of cavities. Your doctor will talk to you about the foods your child eats and how often she rinses her mouth after eating sugary foods. Vegetables, fruits, and whole grains are highly recommended, and processed carbohydrates and foods high in sugar, such as white bread and pastries, are discouraged.

Diet >

By four years old, the dietary requirements for your child differ based on gender and activity levels. Girls between the ages of four and five need between 1,200 and 1,400 calories depending on how active they are, and boys between the ages of four and five need between 1,200 to 1,600 calories depending on their activity levels.

Dietary requirements include:

* grains: 4–5 ounces (half of all grains should be whole grains),
* vegetables: 1–1 ½ cups,
* fruits: 1 ½ cups,
* milk/dairy: 2 cups (milk should be 1% or 2% and fat-free),
* lean meat/beans: 3–4 ounces.

Sharing Reponsibility

A great way to help your child eat healthful foods is to get him involved. Talking about a healthful plate and all the healthful options can help develop cognitive skills.

To ensure diversity in his eating habits, have your child keep a tally of the different foods he has already eaten that day and what foods he still needs.

For example, if your child has cheese and crackers for snack, he can put a check under grains and dairy for the day, leaving him with three other servings of dairy and five more servings of grains for the day. This can be another opportunity to use counting skills and be more engaged in food choices.

Another example is using sorting skills when talking about different colors. Many healthful eating programs for children are encouraging a variety of colors on their plates. Many of the most colorful foods are vegetables and fruits. When at the grocery store, have your child pick fruits and vegetables of different colors or a color you have been talking about. This is a great way to have your child try new healthful foods such as red tomatoes, yellow squash, or purple eggplant. Stay away from unhealthful foods that are high in sugar, which usually come in shades of brown or white.

Cooking together is another great way to get your child involved in what he eats. Matching and gathering the materials needed to cook something and helping measure, stir, and combine ingredients can make eating his healthful creation more exciting.

Think of healthful decorating ideas for the foods you make together. You and your child can use cut up vegetables, raisins, peanut butter, cream cheese, or fruit to make your cooking creation look like a face or an animal.

High-Fiber Foods

Fruits and vegetables are excellent sources of fiber, so you should try to encourage your child to eat these foods. Other foods include beans, whole grain breads, and healthful cereals. One way to find foods that are high in fiber is to read the food labels. You can also teach your child how to read the labels by simply looking for numbers that you suggest he find.

Here is a list of other high-fiber foods that are over five grams: barley, navy beans, baked beans, split peas, lentils, wheat flour, refried beans, prunes, and spinach, just to name a few. Many of these foods may be new to your child, so show them to your child before you cook them and let your child learn a little about each food. Remember, you want to help that picky eater consume high-fiber foods.

Activity Level

It is recommended that children of this age get at least 60 minutes of structured physical activity per day, which means activities led by an adult or parent, and at least 60 minutes of unstructured physical activity such as free play each day. **Structured activities are great for working on sensory motor skills such as throwing, catching, kicking, or pedaling a bike.** Structured activities can also provide moments to practice balance and coordination through games like freeze tag, jumping, or balancing on one foot.

At age four, your child is starting to have his own interests, and this is a good time to enroll him in some extracurricular classes such as dance or team sports. He can have some structured activities planned while also socializing with other children who share the same interests.

Health Visit >

Medical professionals recommend that you bring your child in once a year around his birthday for a regular visit to keep him healthy. You can choose a primary care physician (family doctor) or a pediatrician.

Your doctor will communicate more with your child at this age and bring him into the conversation about safety and his daily routine. The doctor will ask questions about what your child likes to do, his favorite color, and how old he is. If your child is shy, try taking the lead on asking the questions after the doctor to see if your child is more comfortable telling you.

Expectations:

* Your doctor will check your child's vision with a vision test, which will focus more on sight than eye development.

* Your doctor will give your child a hearing exam.

* Your doctor will talk about your child's social and communication skills and ask him questions to hear how he answers. If your child is shy, tell your doctor so that you can ask your child the questions.

* Test your child's balance by having him walk heel to toe in a straight line and balance on one leg.

* Talk about your child's eating habits and physical movement.

* Your doctor will give any vaccines that are due. Vaccines protect your child by immunizing him against certain diseases. Many of these vaccines protect your child for life. Some are given as one shot or a series of shots. When possible your doctor will combine them.

Growing Pains

Growing pains are common among children ages four to six and again between eight and 12 years of age. Growing pains are cramping, achy muscle pains that some children feel in both legs and that keep your child awake at night because the pain usually occurs in the late afternoon or evenings.

Growing pains usually affect the muscles of your child's thighs, calves, and behind the knees. Pain varies from child to child, and most children do not have pain every day. Growing pains are not associated with bone growth but occur more often after your child has an active day of jumping or running.

Did you know that despite the name "growing pains," there is no evidence that growing pains are linked to growth spurts. In fact they simply may be due to intense childhood activities that wear out your child's muscles.

Growing Pains versus Other Pain

Growing pains are different than other medical pain because children respond differently to growing pains. They are more willing to let their parents hold them and massage the parts of their body that hurt when it comes to growing pains.

Help your child by:

* massaging the areas that hurt,
* stretching,
* placing a heating pad on areas that hurt,
* giving the proper dose of children's ibuprofen or acetaminophen.

Routine >

Building a weekly routine for your child helps establish his sleeping and eating schedule, as well as helping him build a better concept of time. Your four year old makes connections based on what he experiences. For example, if you pick up your child from school every day after lunch, that is when he will be expecting you.

Your child is building a better understanding of time. While he cannot yet tell time, he understands basic ideas such as tomorrow, yesterday, and what part of the day something will happen. You can build on these skills by having a weekly calendar for your child that shows what day it is and what is happening that day. You can have him place pictures and words on the calendar and together talk about what events and activities occur each day.

Safety

Safety is even more important for your child during this age because he has developed more gross motor skills. He is also ready and willing to challenge his gross motor abilities and this will result in frequent injuries. Your child is riding a tricycle, running, jumping, and climbing with ease.

Traffic and street safety:

Do not have your child play near streets, and talk to your child about not chasing any balls or toys if they go into the street. Your child should play in a fenced yard or playground with a barrier between him and traffic. Driveways are also dangerous. Walk behind your car before you back out of your driveway to be sure your child is not behind the car. You may not see your child in the rear view mirror. Encourage children to walk in front of the car when they get out so you can always see them.

Strangers:

Four years old is an important time to start talking about strangers. Talk to your child about what to do if someone he doesn't know approaches him. Let him know that if a stranger approaches him, he should start yelling and run, immediately tell you or his caregiver, and not take anything that a stranger gives him.

Playground equipment:

Before letting your child explore the playground, take a walk around the park and check the equipment to make sure the surface under the play equipment is soft enough to absorb a fall. Look for things like shredded rubber, sand, and woodchips or bark; loose filler should be at least nine inches deep under the play equipment. Have your child in sight so that you can monitor how high he climbs on the playground equipment.

Helmet:

Have your child wear a helmet when riding his tricycle, using a scooter, or skating. Some four year olds have transitioned out of a tricycle and can ride a bicycle. Make sure that your child is refitted for a helmet to insure that the brain is protected.

Chemicals:

Keep chemicals and cleaning solutions out of reach.

Car seats:

Four year olds still need a car seat every time they are in the car. The safest place for all children to ride is in the back seat. **At four years of age your child will likely still be in a forward-facing car seat and not yet a booster.** It is important to follow the recommended weight and height requirements for each car seat. And each state has its own age, weight, and height requirements for when it is safe to transition out of a booster into a regular seatbelt or be safe in the front seat.

Mind and Body >
Sexuality, Diversity and Differences, Difficult Conversations, Yoga

Sexuality

Around age four, your child will begin understanding what behaviors and language are used more frequently in private versus in public. **Because your child is used to exploring the world around him and learning by investigating and exploring, be prepared for him to be just as curious about behaviors such as sex and gender differences.**

Children generally don't become modest until about age six, but they will begin around age four to under-stand that there are certain things done in private, such as going to the bathroom and dressing or undressing. Just like they have curiosity about how trees grow, they begin to exhibit curiosity by asking questions about where babies come from, attempting to see other people naked or undressed, and asking about their private parts and their bodily functions.

Don't ignore or jump to conclu-sions when your child asks you questions about sexuality.

You want him to feel comfortable asking you these questions. Approach the questions calmly. You do not want to embarrass your child or ignore him. Ask open-ended questions and guide your child regarding sexual behaviors you may see him engaging in.

Give your child basic information and answers to his questions.

Explain that boys and girls differ. Tell your child that girls' and boys' bodies are different and start to change more when they get older. Give simple explanations about where babies come from. Inform your child that some things are done in private.

Do not make your child feel ashamed about being curious, but it is very important to teach him about personal boundaries.

He may also pick up on "naughty" words that are not appropriate for him to use. Approach your child's use of bad words calmly. Do not laugh or ignore your child using words that are inappropriate, whether they are curse words, sexual words, or potty words. Approach the conversation in a calm manner. The more you make a big deal about it, the more he'll remember and use a word you wish he would not.

Diversity and Differences

Your child is interacting with other children and noticing more of their differences, from gender to race and different abilities. Just like they do when sorting colors and toys, children begin to make connections between people and their differences. It is important to talk to your child about similarities beyond race, such as hair color, the type of shoes people wear, or how many fingers people have, so that he is aware of cultural diversity in a broader context and understands that all people have similarities and differences beyond just culture and skin color.

Tips for helping your child be culturally aware include:

* **Nurture a sense of pride in your child.**

Talk to your child about differences, that differences in people do exist, and that differences are not bad. Look at the positive in some of the differences your child notices in others.

If your child is discouraged about not being able to do something as well as another child, such as running or drawing, remind him of all the things he can do well. If he is embarrassed by his own culture, talk about those differences in a positive manner. For example, say, "Our holiday has these delicious foods, and we get to spend time with our family."

* **Teach your child positive words to associate with differences.**

Instead of describing a difference in another as "not normal" say that it is "not common." Use *different abilities* instead of *disabilities*. Your child is naturally curious, so do not make him feel uncomfortable around someone new. **When you notice your child staring, ask him what he is thinking. Talk to him about the person in the wheelchair or someone of a different race or someone wearing a garment he hasn't seen before.**

If there is someone in your family or a close friend who is from a different culture, let your child ask this person questions. Instead of avoiding the person, talk to your child about being polite. He shouldn't point or stare at anyone. **Giving your child these guidelines also helps him see that everyone is different, and we should treat everyone with respect.**

* **Teach your child the golden rule.**

The golden rule is most commonly known as "treat others as you want to be treated." Talk to your child about how he would feel if he were left out of a group or were told he was not allowed to play because of the shoes he wore that day. Tell him it is okay to have friends you like to play with more than others and that sometimes it is okay to say no to someone who asks to play, but there is a nice way to say it.

Difficult Conversations

When talking to your child about some bad news (like divorce or death), or a big change (such as moving), pick a good time when he is not tired or moody. Ask him what he thinks and how he feels after hearing the news. Ask him again later after he has more time to process the news. Don't be surprised if your young child asks you about it again many days later.

If you have more than one child, make sure you take some time to talk to each child individually. Children of different ages process information in different ways.

Start your conversations with yes and no questions to get the dialogue going.

Be sure not to place blame on anyone or anything in the conversation.

Sometimes young children will change the subject to something that matters more to them at the time, such as asking what is for snack or a question about school. This is okay and is expected. Don't force him to stay on topic because it can frustrate him. Wait for another opportunity to talk about it.

Inform your child's teacher or babysitter that something is happening at home that is out of the ordinary (for example, a parent moving out, a parent traveling, or a death in the family) and ask the sitter or teacher to take some notes on your child's behavior. Your child may act out for attention at school if you are concentrating on the situation at home and not on him. Children can sense when something is wrong and may be confused and keep to themselves or act out either reaction is normal. Be sure to engage your child during times of change so that he does not withdraw emotionally or socially.

Yoga

Having your child participate in yoga gives him the ability to exercise both his body and mind.

Yoga encompasses the whole child by both strengthening children's bodies and calming their minds to shape better focus and build self-confidence. Through yoga, children are able to develop and foster more than just physical skills.

Yoga helps your child build problem-solving skills when testing his balance. Children will try to move their bodies and muscles in different ways until they find the best way to achieve the positions.

Yoga also helps his imagination and creativity skills. You can turn yoga into a story with your child and build language skills by having him name and sequence positions that go along with a storyline. Most of all enjoy your time together.

1. Seesaw

Either siblings or you and your child can practice the seesaw together to stretch the lower back, arms, shoulders, and hamstrings. To do this pose sit across from each other with legs stretched in front of you in a V shape with a tall back. The smaller member of the pair puts his or her legs on the inside of the longer-legged person's legs. Holding hands, gently rock back and forth.

2. Puppy Friends

You and your child (or siblings) should stand facing each other; slowly place your hands on one another's shoulders. Then step back and bend forward at the hips, bringing the head down to rest between the arms. Inhale and exhale several times. Puppy friends will stretch the hamstrings.

3. Holding Hands

You and your child (or siblings) should stand with your backs to each other about a foot apart from one another. Bend over and touch your toes, reach through your legs, and grab each other's hands. Hold hands together as you inhale and exhale several times.

1. Seesaw

2. Puppy Friends

**Remember,
the Whole Child
Parenting Program**
offers appropriate developmental
products and monthly activity books
that walk you through supporting
your child's skills. Using these in
conjunction with the recommended
age-appropriate room
materials ensures faster
development.

3. Holding Hands

Reaching Milestones >

Providing your child with opportunities to develop fully will be the most important gift you can give him during his fourth year. Development in all six categories, especially in the first years of your child's life, helps to maximize his likelihood of getting a good start on his future educational goals.

Monitoring your child's development in the first five years is of the utmost importance, since this is the stage of life when nerve tissue grows the fastest and matures—and is able to take in information. Development monitoring includes all activities related to the promotion of development in your child. Montoring is a flexible, ongoing process.

Use these milestones as a general guide; they are not all-inclusive. Reaching a milestone later does not mean there is a problem. It simply means he needs more time and practice to master the skills.

COGNITIVE

- Sorts objects by size, and by what kind of things they are, e.g. animals, or by color or shape. Can string large beads to make a pattern.
- Compares two weights to work out which is heavier.
- Can count to 10, recognize written numerals, and say numbers up to 20.
- Knows some variations of circle, square, triangle, and rectangle. Can copy shapes like a square, a cross, circle, and a triangle by age five.
- Understands *taller*, *smaller*, and *shorter*, but is still working on arranging a group of things in order of *smallest* to *biggest*.
- Can make observations, gather information, identify patterns, describe and discuss observations.

SOCIAL-EMOTIONAL

- Learns to understand others' feelings and needs, and shows that he can feel empathy for others. More consistently shares and takes turns.
- Learns to better manage intense emotions with coping strategies like talking it out or drawing a picture.
- Can smoothly join in a group play situation and suggest ways to resolve conflict.
- He can make friends and organize games. Sometimes behavior can be "over the top" noisy and exuberant. He may have an imaginary playmate. This is more likely if he doesn't have other children to play with.
- Sense of humor is developing, and he will laugh at a funny situation.

LANGUAGE

- Can understand two or three simple directions to do at once, e.g. "Get your sister's sippy cup, take it to her, and then bring the bowl back to the kitchen."

- Holds a pencil in a mature grip using his preferred hand and can cut on a line.

- Can tell long stories which may be partly true and partly made up. Understands adjectives, adverbs, and some prepositions; uses plurals.

- Understands that letters represent the sounds in spoken words and may associate some letters with their sounds. Recognizes some words he will see a lot, e.g. *stop* on stop signs.

- Capable of writing some legible letters and knows that writing goes from left to right and top to bottom.

CREATIVE

- Can identify changes in pitch, tempo, loudness, and musical duration. Can "sing" songs of his own creation as well as memorized ones.

- Begins to be more realistic and may incorporate letters in his art. Draws a person with identifiable parts.

- Loves to dance and is able to move rhythmically and smoothly.

- His dramatic play is highly imaginative and has the structure of specific scenarios, like going to the grocery store or rescuing a cat stuck in a tree.

PHYSICAL

- Climbs ladders and trees. Stands on tiptoes and walks and runs on tiptoe.

- Runs quite fast and jumps on one foot.

- Can walk along a line for short distances, ride bicycles with or without training wheels.

- Can hop, skip, and gallop. Stands on each foot for three seconds.

HEALTH AND CARE

- Uses a spoon and fork.

- Dresses without help, except with fasteners/buttons.

- Washes self in bathtub.

- Brushes teeth independently.

- Washes and dries hands.

Environment >
Four Year Old's Room

Your four year old is curious and inquisitive, and she wants ample opportunities to be an active participant in her own learning. Every four year old should learn through play. Natural settings like the home offer your child unlimited opportunities to explore and investigate.

A good home learning environment offers a variety of play experiences as well as different types of activities that will encourage her creativity, support language skills, and inspire all of her pretend play ideas.

It is necessary to follow specific steps when setting up a home learning environment for your child.

The first way to create a flexible learning environment that accommodates her needs and interests is to take an inventory of your space and get organized. Remove any clutter, like old toys, from the room.

Store all learning materials in your **Six Drawer Whole Child Color-Coded Organizer.**

Then place the recommended furniture in her room for her to use in a variety of activities. She will be able to choose based on the **six areas of development: cognitive, social emotional, language, creative, physical, and health.**

The following picture gives you a glimpse of what your four year old's room will look like after you have followed the steps above.

Whole Child: Four Year Old's Room

The following list contains must-have items for your four year old's room. These items will be used interchangeably with your other Whole Child Parenting materials.

1. Six Drawer Whole Child Color-Coded Organizer
2. Whole Child Wall Planner
3. Table and Chairs
4. Easel
5. Carpet
6. Puppet/Pretend Play Materials
7. Kitchen Set
8. Blocks and Manipulatives
9. Bookshelf

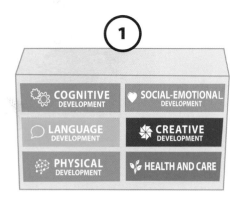

1. Six Drawer Whole Child Color-Coded Organizer

Easily organize educational materials and toys by six areas of development. Ensure your child always has enough materials in each drawer.

2. Whole Child Wall Planner

Plan and organize weekly activities based on six areas of development.

3. Table and Chairs

Provides a clearly defined space, at child's level and shaped to support posture, for child to work independently and stay focused. Use for fine motor development and learning shapes, colors, spatial concepts, science, letters, and numbers.

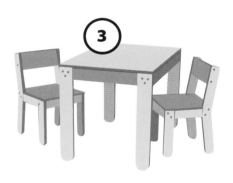

4. Easel

Provides a place for child to play with well-organized art materials displayed at eye level. Materials are easily changed out by child with help or by parent. Use for fostering development of child's aesthetic sense and for engaging in creative experiences.

5. Carpet

Provides a soft, safe place, free from clutter, for your child to play on. Use for providing materials in one central location at child's eye level. Enables parent to change out materials and still maintain child safety.

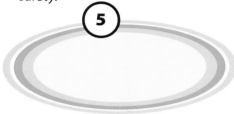

6. Puppet/Pretend Play Materials

Helps social communication, and interactive skills through shared experiences. Use for pretend play and peek-a-boo games.

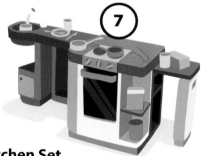

7. Kitchen Set

Organize props and pretend food. Can be easily rotated in and out. Use to develop self-help skills, independence, and imagination.

8. Blocks and Manipulatives

Use for construction and spatial skill development while talking about shapes, sizes, colors. Helps develop recognition, counting, sorting, and matching skills.

9. Bookshelf

Makes books easily accessible to child and supports independent exploration and literacy skills. Use for bonding with child through one-on-one time.

whole child activity books >

Have a look at a sample of our series of activity books for four year olds. This series of 12 titles helps four year olds exercise their brains and bodies in every category of development explored in the Whole Child Parenting books. The 12 titles are available now.

WHOLE CHILD

Activity Book

Age 4

Transportation

WHOLE CHILD = $\dfrac{\text{smart} + \text{creative}}{\text{healthy} + \text{happy}}$

COGNITIVE
DEVELOPMENT

Problem-solving · Attention · Numbers

SOCIAL-EMOTIONAL
DEVELOPMENT

Self-control · Friendship · Feelings

LANGUAGE
DEVELOPMENT

Communication · Speaking · Literacy

CREATIVE
DEVELOPMENT

Dramatic Play · Dance · Music · Arts

PHYSICAL
DEVELOPMENT

Motor Skills: Sensory, Gross, Fine

HEALTH AND CARE

Hygiene · Diet · Routine · Yoga

sneak peek >

TRAIN

DISCOVERY

The following activities are all about trains. Read this information aloud to your child. Say the word *train* aloud as you point to the word. Ask your child to point to one thing on the train she would like to learn more about (the wheels or the cowcatcher). This will further enrich your discussions about trains.

Look around your house together and peek inside your activity box to collect up to five items that are related to trains such as books, stickers, toys, cargo, etc.

WHAT DO TRAINS DO?

Chugging across a track, trains are an important form of transportation all over the world. Trains have passenger cars to hold people. Some trains also have sleeper cars for people who take very long trips. Trains can have cargo cars that carry everything from livestock like cows and pigs to boxes filled with supplies or food and more.

FUN FACTS

Did you know all trains have an engineer? The engineer is the person who drives the train. He will make the train go quickly or slowly.

sneak peek >

1

 # EARLY MATH SKILLS

DISCOVER!

Four year olds are learning to observe objects with curiosity and notice differences, such as how a circle is round and how a square has straight sides. Your child uses his knowledge of spatial relationships to think logically to see how objects can be classified based upon size. Your child is also able to trace and count numbers.

DID YOU KNOW?

Providing opportunities for your child to develop a further understanding of spatial concepts is easy. Try building with blocks and observing objects from different viewpoints. Talk about spatial concepts such as *full* and *empty*, *high* and *low* as you do this.

LET'S DO MORE!

In your home, have your child find four items that are the same shape. Then ask him to tell you what other characteristics the four items might have in common, such as their color or size.

CIRCLES AND SQUARES

Skill • Recognizing shapes

Directions: Have your child use a pencil to trace the circle and square under the train. Then have him connect the dots to draw in the rest of the circle and square below that are missing the other half. Have him pencil in all four shapes.

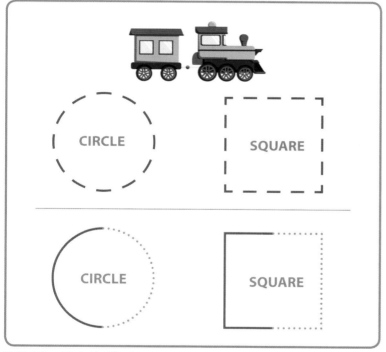

 Being able to identify shapes will help your child sort objects and describe objects based on their shape, for example, a square napkin.

7

LETTER C

Directions: Have your child look at the letter C at the top of the page and say "C." Point to the word *car* and say, "C, KUH, car." Ask her to use a pencil to trace the letter C on the first row. Then have her practice writing the letter C on the empty line below.

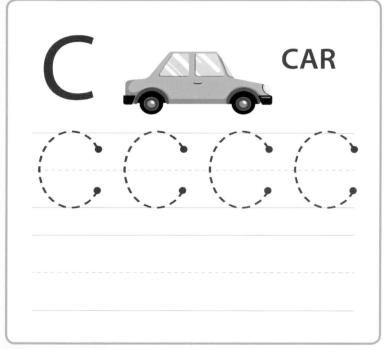

Tracing the letter C is an easy way for your child to learn to write the letter and is an important step toward freehand writing.

LETTER C

Skill · Recognizing letter sounds

Directions: Have your child say the name of each picture. Have her draw a circle around the C in each name using a pencil. Then ask her to draw a line under the object that someone can drive.

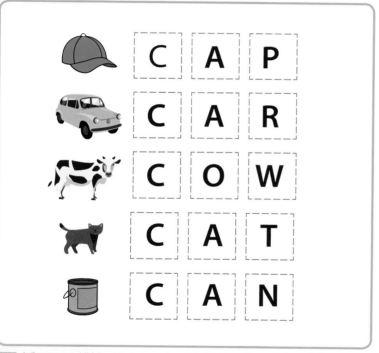

When your child is able to identify printed letters like a C she will then be able to distinguish between different letters like a G, despite their similar appearance.

35

sneak peek >

2

EMOTIONAL DEVELOPMENT

DISCOVER!

Your four year old understands that she is a person separate from others. Besides seeing differences in her physical appearance, like her hair color, she is also seeing that there are differences in how others feel and do things.

DID YOU KNOW?

Your child will notice that just because she likes planes does not mean that her friend does. She will also make these connections with her abilities when she notices that she can ride a bike, but her friend is still learning how.

LET'S DO MORE!

Talk to your child about things that make her similar as well as different from others. Helping her understand her place in the family leads to her being a confident member of her community. She can see that she belongs, as well as what she can bring to the table, and what makes her special.

CREATIVE DEVELOPMENT  **PHYSICAL** DEVELOPMENT  **HEALTH AND CARE**

ABOUT ME

Skill · Recognizing hair color

Directions: Look in a mirror with your child. Point out your own hair color and your child's. Using whatever crayons she likes, have her draw in the hair color for the boy and the girl.

Being able to recognize that there are different hair colors leads to your child learning more about diversity and how there are different feelings, cultures, and abilities.

sneak peek >

CREATIVE
DEVELOPMENT

COLORING

Skill · Developing creativity

Directions: Get out a blue, yellow, and green crayon. Have her color the plane picture according to what number and color that is on the key below.

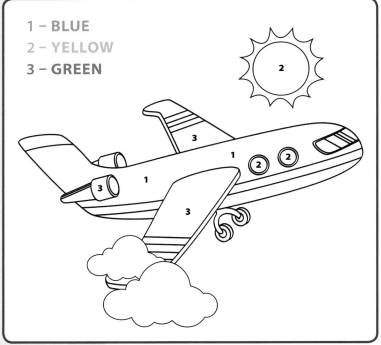

1 – **BLUE**
2 – YELLOW
3 – **GREEN**

Enabling your child to use more than one color when coloring allows her to express herself by creating more detailed and elaborate art.

58

CREATIVE DEVELOPMENT

PAPER AIRPLANES

Skill · Rhyming

Directions: Read the rhyme below to your child. Have her color the paper airplanes.

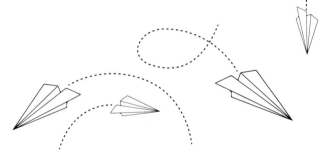

Four paper airplanes all around,
(Hold up four fingers.)
they start out slowly from the ground.
(Slowly bring hand up from the ground.)

Some go fast; some go slow.
(Move hand fast, then slowly.)
They fly up high, then zoom down low.
(Fly hand up, then down.)

 Making rhymes part of your daily routine helps your child transition from one activity to another.

sneak peek >

DEVELOPING MOTOR SKILLS

DISCOVER!

Your child has better strength and coordination now, which will give him the confidence he needs to try more challenging gross motor skills. At or about age four he is able to catch and throw objects (ball) or stretch out his arms and keep them up in that position for a brief period of time. This leads to developing stronger shoulder and arm muscles, as well as sharpening his hand-eye coordination skills and quick response skills as he responds to an object like a ball being thrown in his direction.

DID YOU KNOW?

Strong arm muscles will help your child with day-to-day tasks such as lifting a backpack or other items that have a little weight. It will also enhance his ability to climb on a jungle gym.

LET'S DO MORE!

Help build your child's shoulder strength by playing a game. Tell your child the wall is falling down, and he has to push as hard as he can against the wall to keep it from falling down. This activity will not only strengthen the muscles but will also improve his stability.

5

STRECHING ARMS

Skill · Learning to move arms

Directions: Ask your child to stretch out his arms. Have your child raise his arms up to his shoulders. Read the chant below while your child flies around the house.

I'm a little airplane.
Now watch me fly!
Lifting off the runway
up in the sky.

 When the large muscles of the shoulder work effectively together, they provide stability for the smaller muscles in the arms and hands so they can do their job as well.

Whole Child Activity Books:
Transportation Age Four
Available now >

WHOLE CHILD

Parenting Program books and materials are available worldwide.

The book that kick started the program!

Also available separately

Whole Child Program Activity Books

- 4 **Infant** Titles
- 6 **Toddler** Titles
- 12 **Age Two** Titles
- 12 **Age Three** Titles
- 12 **Age Four** Titles

Whole Child Program books and materials are available at special discounts when purchased in bulk for premiums and sales promotions as well as for fundraising or educational use. For details, please contact us at: sales@wholechild.co

Visit us on the web at: www.wholechild.co